THE OUTSIDER

A Play in Three Acts

hany's
ene in Act II.

BY

DOROTHY BRANDON

(*Leon M. Lion's Production*)

COPYRIGHT, 1926, BY SAMUEL FRENCH, LTD.

Producer's Book.

<table>
<tr><td>LONDON
SAMUEL FRENCH, LTD.
PUBLISHERS
26 SOUTHAMPTON STREET
STRAND, W.C.2</td><td>NEW YORK
SAMUEL FRENCH
PUBLISHER
25 WEST 45TH STREET</td></tr>
</table>

The fee for the representation of this play by amateurs is Five Guineas, payable in advance to—

Messrs. Samuel French, Ltd.,
26 Southampton Street,
Strand, London, W.C.2,

or their authorized agents, who, upon payment of the fee, will issue a licence for the performance to take place.

No performance may be given unless this licence has been obtained.

In the event of further performances being given the fee for each and every representation subsequent to the first is Four Guineas. This reduction applies only in the case of the performances being consecutive and at the same theatre or hall.

Character Costumes and Wigs used in the performance of plays contained in French's Acting Edition may be obtained from Messrs. CHARLES H. FOX, Ltd., Acre House, 72 Long Acre, London, W.C.2.

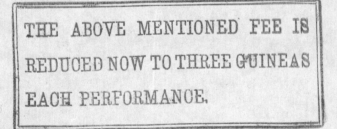

THE ABOVE MENTIONED FEE IS REDUCED NOW TO THREE GUINEAS EACH PERFORMANCE.

Made and Printed in Great Britain by Butler & Tanner Ltd., Frome and London

ST. JAMES'S THEATRE

KING STREET, ST. JAMES'S STREET, S.W.

By arrangement with GILBERT MILLER.

FRIDAY EVENING, JUNE 1st, 1923, at 8.30.

FRANK CURZON and LEON M. LION

PRESENT

LESLIE FABER AND ISOBEL ELSOM

IN

"THE OUTSIDER"

A Play in Three Acts by DOROTHY BRANDON.

ANTON RAGATZY	.	*Leslie Faber.*
JASPER STURDEE, M.S.	.	*Dawson Milward.*
SIR MONTAGUE TOLLEMACHE ⎞		*E. Lyall Swete.*
SIR NATHAN ISRAEL ⎬ F.R.C.S. ⎨ . . .		*Randolph McLeod.*
VINCENT HELMORE ⎠		*Charles Kenyon.*
FREDERICK LADD	.	*Cecil Fowler.*
BASIL OWEN	.	*Evan Thomas.*
MADAME KLOST	.	*Stella Rho.*
PRITCHARD	.	*Ruth Maitland.*
LALAGE STURDEE	.	*Isobel Elsom.*

ACT I. Scene—The Honorary Staff's Room at St. Martha's Hospital, S.E.

ACT II. Scene—LALAGE's Music Room, Harley Street.
(Time—Next Day.)

ACT III. Scene 1—LALAGE's Flat, Regent's Park.
(Time—Four months later. Evening.)

The Curtain is lowered for One Minute between Scenes 1 and 2 to denote the passage of time.

Scene 2—The same.

(Time—Eight Months later. Morning.)

TIME—THE PRESENT.

The Play produced by LEON M. LION.

To face page 5]

" THE OUTSIDER "

ACT I

(NOTE *to Producers.—Keep this whole Act brisk and cheerful and play for every ounce of comedy, except in* STURDEE'S *scenes and* LALAGE'S.)

SCENE.—*The Honorary Staff's Room at St. Martha's Hospital, S.E.*

(TOLLEMACHE, *an upright, well-preserved man of about 65, obstinate, intellectual, not easily moved, is sitting in the arm-chair on hearth, and* SIR NATHAN ISRAEL *is standing by the mantelpiece listening to* LADD, *who has just finished speaking heatedly and energetically. He is a man about 40, with a clever head, but rather a disappointing chin. Full of nervous energy but lacking real force.* ISRAEL *is a tall thin Jew, the very highest type of refined intellectuality. He is probably about 45, for his hair is beginning to be tinged with a grey. Both he and* TOLLEMACHE *have the air of listening very carefully to what* LADD *is saying without being in the least convinced by it.*)

LADD. And those are facts! (*He speaks with a strong Scotch or Provincial accent. Throughout the Scene, he has the deadly pertinacity of the lesser man trying to convince the greater by incontrovertible statement.*)

TOLLEMACHE. Yes. (*Chuckling.*) But the question is—will Sturdee consent to meet him ?

HELMORE (*entering* R.U.E.). Meet who ? (*Lights cigarette.*)

(*He comes down* C. *A short, broad man with a heavy smooth face, but quick, beautifully sympathetic eyes. Rather like a pale intellectual schoolboy with a lined, tired countenance. He affects the cynical blasé air of a society entertainer and is far more entertaining than most of them.*)

LADD (*pause*). Ragatzy.

HELMORE (*with a little snort*). I should say not.

ISRAEL (*with a slight accent*). That is what I think, Helmore.

TOLLEMACHE (C. *just* L. *of table*). You know what Sturdee is, Ladd.

HELMORE. So massively upright, that when he lived in Great Cumberland Place the nurses here used to say he ought to take the title Lord Marble Arch.

5

ISRAEL. Ah, but he is human, very dear and human.

HELMORE. Not to outsiders. And this blackguard Ragatzy is one in every sense of the word.

TOLLEMACHE (*choleric and indignant*). Ladd wants to bring him inside. (*Snorts. He is the hard shell reactionary, fighting all new and unorthodox methods.*)

HELMORE. Does he ? Why ? (*Turns to* LADD.)

LADD (*facing* HELMORE—*with nervous force*). Because his invention, the Ragatzy Rack, has cured cases we've pronounced incurable. There's a woman we had at this hospital . . .

TOLLEMACHE (*to* LADD). My dear Ladd, *all* these unqualified practitioners cure incurable cases. No one would ever hear of 'em if they didn't.

HELMORE. There is more joy in Fleet Street over one cripple cured by a charlatan than ninety-and-nine put right by qualified surgeons. Because the fat fool public likes to go to quacks. It's an awfully big adventure.

TOLLEMACHE. All the poor wretches who want so badly to believe in God only they haven't got the faith, are waiting for a miracle with their souls wide open.

(LADD *crosses to bureau* L. *and sits.*)

ISRAEL (L.). I think the public have a conviction that the reason why the Christ was able to perform miracles was because he was *not* a Fellow of the Royal College of Surgeons.

HELMORE (L.). He'd never have founded a religion on the strength of His miracles if He had been. They'd have said they weren't miracles. (*Crosses up* C. *to bureau and has back to audience.*)

ISRAEL. It is the same with Ragatzy.

TOLLEMACHE. Look here, Israel, I know you don't mean to be blasphemous, but if you're going to compare Ragatzy . . . a cheap-jack charlatan . . . (*Rises and moves up stage to window.*)

HELMORE (*facing* TOLLEMACHE). Cheap. . . . Do you know what he charges ?

TOLLEMACHE (*returns to* R. *of table—testily*). I said cheap-jack, not cheap. Of course the fellow's out to make money. That's why he calls his apparatus the Ragatzy Rack. It's a catch word. And it's the brutal audacity of it that catches 'em. It *is* a Rack.

LADD. That stretches out and straightens crooked limbs.

HELMORE. But we should have camouflaged it as—(*reeling it off with mocking rapid rhythm*)—a perambulatory, automatic, electrical extension for the reduction of femoral congenital dislocation and lateral curvature. And no one would ever have mentioned it in polite society !

TOLLEMACHE. This damn alien calls himself an American citizen, doesn't he ?

HELMORE. What is he by birth, not nationalization ?

LADD. A Czech or Slovak of some sort.

TOLLEMACHE. Anyway, something mongrel from middle Europe.

ISRAEL. Arrived viâ New York. A hybrid American, who . . .

TOLLEMACHE. Is the worst of the old world and new . . . *and* new. . . .

HELMORE (*coming down* C.). Oh, I say, we're making a Limerick.
 "He's a hybrid American who,
  Is the worst of the Old World and New——"
(*Carry-on.*) "He's the swank of a Yank——"

ISRAEL. "And the *push* of a Tank."

TOLLEMACHE. "A downright disgusting Yahoo." That's got him. (*Moves to the mantelpiece and stands leaning on it.*)

(HELMORE *moves up stage to window, where he stands lighting a cigar.*)

LADD. Look here, Tollie, the man's not as bad as all that. I admit his manner is offensive and he's a bit of an extortioner . . . but he does cure people.

(*Enter* STURDEE R.)

STURDEE. Who does? *Stay in doorway.*

(*He is a handsome grey-haired man of* 60, *upright, dignified and erect, with a noble head and kind, keen humorous eyes. His tall splendid figure is very effectively set off by his well-cut morning coat, as he comes* C., *tapping his eyeglasses* [*pince-nez*] *on his other hand.*)

LADD (*pause*). Ragatzy.

STURDEE (*standing in doorway—pause. Simply, but with weight*). He ought not to be allowed to.

LADD. Not to be allowed to cure people.

STURDEE. No. Not without the knowledge that will give them a reasonable security that he won't either kill or cripple them. What is he? A surgical-instrument maker . . . a mechanic. (STURDEE *drops* C.)

(LADD *drops* D.L. *to bureau.*)

LADD. He's an absolute master of the mechanism of the human body.

STURDEE. Who taught him? Who certified him? Where did he study anatomy . . . or learn surgery?

LADD. *He* taught himself.

STURDEE. And certifies himself. And yet there are people so foolish that they allow this man to treat them without a surgeon.

LADD. Most successfully.

STURDEE. We hear of his successes, but we don't hear of his failures. (*A look passes between* HELMORE *and* NATHAN.) People only blare out about it when a qualified surgeon fails to cure them. But when some wretched charlatan makes them worse they keep

Goes to sit right of table.

a very still tongue in their heads, for fear their friends should say,
" What fools you were to go to him." (*Goes to table and sits* R. *of
it.*)

TOLLEMACHE)   (Hear ! Hear !
ISRAEL   } (*together*). { You are absolutely right.
HELMORE   )   (I quite agree with you.

STURDEE. I am glad you agree with me. (*Facing round again.*)
Do you hold a brief for this fellow, Ladd ?

LADD. Aye.

STURDEE. You do ! Why ?

upon → LADD (*pertinaciously*). Because he does cures. Amazing cures.
(*Moves* C.)

HELMORE. So do Pale Pills for Pink People. . . . According to
their own advertisement ! (*Sits in chair by window.*)

(STURDEE *moves up stage to bureau.*)

LADD (*moving a little up to* STURDEE, L.C.). Listen please ! I
had a case . . . a boy of ten. I told the mother—a very rich woman
who would have paid anything—that nothing could be done. He
would never walk without crutches. She went away.

ISRAEL. Aha . . . to Ragatzy. . . .

(STURDEE *sits at bureau.*)

LADD. Exactly. . . . But she came back to me because Ragatzy
told her if she would let the boy be put on the Rack for six months
he would have him walking alone, but she was afraid to have it done
without a surgeon. She wept.

TOLLEMACHE. Good Heavens ! Ladd ! surely you're used to
mother's tears ?

STURDEE (*quietly*). I'm not.

LADD. She implored me to take the case, because Ragatzy had
said he was willing to work under me. I didn't hear till afterwards
that he had told her, if she would pay him a thousand pounds—
(*general movement of doctors*—HELMORE *laughs*) . . . he was willing
to allow any qualified fool to look on while he did the work.

STURDEE. Typical.

HELMORE. That is Ragatzy.

LADD. In six months' time the boy was walking entirely without
support . . . and without a limp. *That*—is also Ragatzy. . . .

HELMORE. Damn him !

LADD (*moving* L. *towards bureau*). I admit I was impressed and
told him so . . . then the fellow grinned like a dog and said I might
superintend any other cases I liked to bring him.

TOLLEMACHE. And after that . . .

HELMORE. Did you ?

LADD. Only hopeless cases, after I had told the relatives the
exact truth and left the decision to them.

STURDEE. Ah! Go on. *(Moving down* C. *and sitting on table* C.*)*

LADD. In the last eighteen months I have sent him eleven cases.
Two he has failed with. . . .

STURDEE. Was one of them Captain Wycherly?

LADD. Aye. How do you know about him?

STURDEE (*to the three surgeons*). He came to see me yesterday
. . . with that power he had left in his wounded leg entirely gone.
Destroyed by this man's treatment.

LADD. He warned him that there was the risk.

STURDEE. It was a certainty. He must have known it was a
sin to touch him.

ISRAEL. And he is one of the two failures.

HELMORE. What about the rest?

LADD. Absolutely cured.

ISRAEL. All children, I suppose?

LADD. Aye.

HELMORE. You can do anything with children.

LADD (*quietly*). None of us could do anything with these children.

HELMORE. Therefore you think that we ought to see him.

LADD. *Aye, and investigate.* (*Tentatively.*)

STURDEE. *See* him. Where?

LADD (*moving* C.) Well, I told him that, if he would come here
to-day—(*look between* HELMORE, TOLLEMACHE *and* NATHAN)—and
bring his rack with him, I would *ask* the surgeons to examine it.

STURDEE. I don't mind doing that.

TOLLEMACHE (*disapproval*). And if we are satisfied—what then?

HELMORE (*rises to fireplace after* TOLLEMACHE *has crossed*). Are
we to meet him? (*At foot of table.*)

ISRAEL. Recognize him?

STURDEE. As what? A surgical-instrument maker—if so, he
must give up taking cases without a surgeon.

LADD. He won't do that. It wouldn't pay him and he'd lose
prestige.

(*General exclamation.*)

TOLLEMACHE. Prestige? Ha!

STURDEE (*moving down* L.). Then he must become a surgeon
himself. Let him walk the hospitals and take the examinations.

LADD. He won't. He says he hasn't the time. (*Sits below
bureau and fills pipe.*)

STURDEE. Then I have no time for *him.* (*Rising up* C.) I am
going to Newcastle to-night to operate early to-morrow. But if I
were not I would leave here before he comes, rather than even seem
to recognize that this pirate surgeon may sail under the flag of his
own skull and cross bones, and plunder, wound and murder as he
goes. None of us must countenance him. None of us. It must

be an absolute boycott. (*He goes to the door, then turns gently.*)
Ladd, if I seem intolerant, I will tell you why. . . .

ISRAEL. No, no. My dear Sturdee——

STURDEE (*almost c.—gently insistent*). Yes. Because I have
learned the mischief that these quacks can do—in the person of
my own daughter—my only child. You know . . . some of you . . .
that my young wife, her mother, died when she was born. But
you do not know that I had then to make the most terrible decision
that can be asked of any man. The doctors came to me and told
me they could not save both mother and child. . . . They asked
me—" Which ? " . . . there could be no question, I said . . .
" Sacrifice the child." It was done. But too late, the mother died.
And the child cried out . . . and lived.

(*Pause.*)

They brought her to me . . . and I would not look at her. I could
not. I thought of her only as the little murderess of her mother. I
had her sent away out of the house, out of my sight, and remem-
brance, to a foster-mother in the country. . . . Then I left England—left my little helpless girl. . . . (*He walks away to the window
and stands looking out for a moment. His perfect stillness is more
terrible than any loss of self-control. He turns back, to top of table.*)

(*The others wait in moved silence.*)

I travelled in the East, I practised in the East, I studied and practised in the States. After much delay, I received an ill-spelt, ill-
written letter from the foster-mother. The child was healthy,
beautiful, remarkably intelligent, but, at nearly three years old,
she could not walk. . . . She still crawled, dragging one little foot.
They were having her treated by the local bone-setter.

(*Exclamation from* TOLLEMACHE " *Oh Good God !* ")

But it seemed no better so they wrote to me. . . . I think I knew
I was a father for the first time, when I heard that my own little
daughter was in the brutal blundering hands. . . . (*Moving down
to* LADD.)

LADD (*in consternation*). Sturdee. . . . I never heard. I never
knew. . . . Please . . . (*Puts his hand as though to stop him.*)

ISRAEL (*very gently*). We understand.

TOLLEMACHE } (*together*). { Yes, indeed.
HELMORE   }   { Yes. Yes, yes——

TOLLEMACHE. Yes.

STURDEE. No. I want to drive it home to you that, before I
could reach her, the child's hip, dislocated at birth, had been so
twisted and torn by this infamous ignoramus, and the joint so
damaged that nothing could be done. . . . My little daughter, who
smiled and dragged herself on to my knee to kiss me, was crippled

for life . . . through my neglect . . . my criminal foregoing of my fatherhood. (*Turns up* C.)

(*Pause.*)

ISRAEL. Sturdee, I think we hardly realize she *is* a cripple.

TOLLEMACHE. Her charm.

HELMORE. Her spirit.

ISRAEL. Her great gift.

STURDEE. Ah. . . . Thank God! She has her music.

(*The door is half opened and* LALAGE STURDEE, *with her hand on the doorknob, appears half revealed in the doorway. A slender girl of about 25 with a lovely intelligent and vivid face, beautifully dressed in a long fur coat and picturesquely fashionable hat, leaning on a crutch in her right hand.*)

LALAGE (*in clear gay, but reproachful tones*). Father! have you quite forgotten me?

STURDEE (*quietly*). Not quite.

LALAGE (*lovingly*). Oh, never quite! (*Tentatively.*) May I come in or are you saying dreadful things I mustn't hear?

STURDEE (*turning away*). No. Come in, Lally.

(*She walks in and with the help of her crutch-stick and by holding herself very upright manages to conceal much of the limp, but even so the tragedy of her life is apparent at every step. She holds crutch in her RIGHT hand and limps with LEFT foot. Her left shoulder drops a little each time she limps because her left hip is too weak to support the weight of her body, which is thrown on to her right hand and crutch when her left foot is on the ground.*)

(LADD *moves up to her.* NATHAN *crosses below table.* HELMORE *above table.*)

LALAGE (*nodding*). How do you do, Mr. Ladd? Dear Sir Montague. Vinc . . . ah, Mr. Helmore. How are you, Sir Nathan?

(*They all press round her. She gives them her left hand, because while she is moving she cannot let go of the crutch in her right.*)

ISRAEL. Come and sit down, Miss Lally?

(*All try to conceal their emotion by being very cheerful and making a great fuss of her.*)

TOLLEMACHE. Yes, by me here, eh? (*Sits* L. *of table; pulls forward chair below table.*)

LALAGE (*rapidly*). No, no I can't. . . . I mustn't. I've only come to fetch him. And he promised that he wouldn't keep me waiting, because I've got a big rehearsal this afternoon.

(*N.B.—When she has to stand a little while, she instinctively shifts the weight of her body on to her right hip.*)

ISRAEL. At the Albert Hall . . .

LALAGE (*proudly*). My new song cycle, Moorland Love Songs. You know those lovely lyrics. . . .

ISRAEL. Basil Owen's ?

LALAGE. Yes. (*Softly.*) Isn't he wonderful ? (*Speaks tenderly as a woman speaks of the man she loves.*)

ISRAEL. They will go well to your music.

LALAGE (*with enthusiasm*). I *think* I've got the sunshine and the freedom.

STURDEE (*proudly putting arm about her shoulders*). And the colour of the gorse and heather. (*Moves up stage and collects papers from bureau.*)

LALAGE (*with intensity*). If *only* the voices and the instruments will bring them out.

TOLLEMACHE. You conduct yourself ?

(HELMORE *nudges* TOLLEMACHE.)

LALAGE (*desperate and passionate*). I can't. *I can't.* That's just what maddens me ! The thing takes nearly half an hour and I can't stand so long without my stick. (*To* LADD.) You see, you must have both hands or you can't command the orchestra. That's why I want to get there early to tell their new conductor exactly what I want. *Can* you come now, father ? (*Turning* L., *moves towards door up* L.)

STURDEE (*gravely*). Yes, my dear, I'm coming.

ISRAEL (*two steps up with her*). Don't worry. You'll find the new man is a real musician.

LALAGE. But he isn't *me* ! Just think how you'd feel if you had to watch another surgeon performing your pet operation.

NATHAN (*moving down a little*). That will come to all of us with the powerlessness of age.

LALAGE. I've never had the power of youth ! (*She catches her breath as though ashamed at the involuntary revelation and looks anxiously round at her father, hoping he has not heard. He makes no sign of emotion, but stands up stage with his back to her. Recovering herself, she waves gaily to the doctors and limps through door.*)

(LALAGE *exits as* ISRAEL *and* TOLLEMACHE *exchange sympathetic glances.* STURDEE *comes across to door and points after her.*)

STURDEE (*quietly*). You see ! (*Emphatic.*) I will not meet this man who in his presumptuous ignorance may do to another man's daughter what has been done to mine. I will *not* meet him. (*He goes off* L., *closing the door after him.*)

(*Pause.*)

(NATHAN *crosses up* C. *to bureau.*)

LADD (*under his breath as the door closes*). But he *does* cure people. (*Lights pipe.*)

HELMORE (*irritably moving towards* LADD). For God's sake, Ladd, don't keep on repeating that! You're as monotonous as a cuckoo. (*Crosses above table to* R.)

ISRAEL (*indignant*). Is it not enough that Sturdee . . .

TOLLEMACHE. Yes. We *must* turn that fellow down.

LADD. If you do, he'll turn up again.

TOLLEMACHE. Will he?

HELMORE. What do you mean? (*Selects magazine from table, sits chair below door* R. *down stage.*)

LADD. He's got a lot of influence behind him. Most of the children he's cured belong to well-known people.

HELMORE (*gloomily*). Half the infant peerage, I presume. . . .

LADD. Then there are the wounded officer cases. They're going to take it up. Several of 'em have got a lot of pull with the Press. And if we don't see him.

HELMORE. There'll be a newspaper campaign against **us.**

TOLLEMACHE. *See* him? After what Sturdee said?

ISRAEL (*who has been pacing to and fro back of stage, drops to* L. *of* SIR MONTAGUE). I think yes, *because* of that. Do not let it be said it is because he has his private feelings against outsiders that he influences us. (*Looking at* LADD. *Walking* L. *of* HELMORE.) Let us see Ragatzy as a body, all together, and explain to him our official attitude. That will be courteous. (*Facing* TOLLEMACHE.) Open-minded. . . . And put us so much in the right. . . .

TOLLEMACHE. He couldn't put us in the wrong. By the by, what *is* our official attitude? (*Rises and replaces chair by table.*)

LADD (*scratching head*). Gosh?

ISRAEL. Either he gives up taking cases without a surgeon, or takes a degree.

TOLLEMACHE. Yes, that's all right. It isn't giving way an inch, but it looks as if it is.

HELMORE (*grumpily*). It's better than a correspondence in " The Times."

ISRAEL. Well, if we're going to see him, we may as well get it over. Is he here, Ladd?

LADD. I'll ask. . . . (*Going to speaking-tube on wall* R. *by door.*) Is that the hall porter? Good. Has Mr. Ragatzy arrived? Rag-at-zy? No . . . what's that? Oh, all right, I know. Yes, yes, she'd better wait down there till he comes. . . . Tell her—tell her.

TOLLEMACHE (*suspiciously*). Who's " she "?

LADD. One of his patients. The woman we had here. Madame Klost.

ISRAEL. An adult?

LADD. Yes. Don't you remember the case . . . a dislocated hip with lameness of fifteen years' standing. We could do nothing for her . . . but . . .

HELMORE (*gloomily*). He's cured her . . . with the Rack . . . and brought her here to tell us so. And be damned to him.

LADD. You see—(*comes down* C.),—as she was turned away from this very hospital by all of us as uncurable . . .

HELMORE. He's going to let us have that in the neck, of course.

LADD. She is a very poor woman and a compatriot of his, so he has treated her for nothing.

TOLLEMACHE (*snorts*). Except advertisement. (*Moves L., sits at table.*)

LADD (*shrugging*). Oh . . . aye . . . of course . . . that.

HELMORE. H'm . . . it wouldn't be a bad idea to have her up before he comes.

LADD. Oh aye ! (*Crosses back to 'phone.*)

HELMORE. I expect he's the blustering, bragging sort of fellow who won't let her say a word for herself.

LADD (*to mouthpiece*). Will you ask the woman who is waiting for Mr. Ragatzy to come up here, please ? Yes, now, at once ! *prop down le*

HELMORE (*going to the door*). I'm going to watch her walking down the corridor. Some of these lame people can go quite well for two or three steps but not for fifty. (*Opens door and looks off* L.)

TOLLEMACHE (*rising and joining* HELMORE *in doorway*). Yes, this thing has got to be tested to the bone, Ladd. We can't simply take your word for it.

ISRAEL (*coming to stand behind them*). You say she could not walk at all without crutches ?

LADD. And then only with great pain and difficulty. (*Takes up position behind* TOLLEMACHE.)

HELMORE (*joins the doctors*). I think I remember her. She was such a poor creature.

LADD. Here she comes. . . . Now watch her.

(*Pause.*)

HELMORE. Look here, Ladd, do you mean to say this is the same woman ?

LADD. You'd better ask her yourself. Come in, madame.

(*Enter* MADAME KLOST, R.U.E. *She is a plain, poorly dressed woman, just a shade above the artisan class. Rather foreign-looking but respectable, honest and nervous. She stands a moment in the doorway.*)

(*Encouragingly.*) Just walk over to the ~~fireplace~~ *screen*, will you ?

(*As she crosses* HELMORE *moves down* L. LADD *down* L.C. TOLLEMACHE *down* R.C. NATHAN R. MADAME *walks across the room, holding herself very erect, very pleased at showing off how slightly she limps. The doctors follow her, watching her very carefully from the side and behind till she reaches the hearthrug, when she turns and looks back at them timidly but expectantly. No one moves till she has spoken, then* TOLLEMACHE ~~sits below~~ table c.)

MADAME KLOST. Is that enough ?

HELMORE (*resentfully*). There's a very great improvement since we last saw you, Madame Klost.

MADAME KLOST (*with satisfaction*). Ah . . . you remember.

HELMORE. I do.

ISRAEL. I also.

TOLLEMACHE. But you still limp.

MADAME KLOST (*eager*). Ah yes, sir, but the after-treatment is not yet finished. For three months more I have to sleep upon the Rack each night.

TOLLEMACHE. Sit down, won't you ? Is it painful ?

(*She sits down* R. *The others stand round questioning her gently and kindly ; but watching her very keenly.*)

MADAME KLOST. No . . . there was no pain to call pain. A little ache perhaps to be kept stretched out and still. Beyond that . . . nothing at all to be compared to the great weariness of walking and the pain. For me to lie down upon the Rack was rest.

TOLLEMACHE. And you're very grateful to Mr. Ragatzy, I suppose ?

MADAME KLOST. Indeed . . . indeed. But I have also not forgotten how you also were so kind to me. You told me so gently and so sorrowfully . . .

ISRAEL. That we could not do you any good.

MADAME KLOST (*to* HELMORE). Yes . . . and you, sir, came after me and gave me money.

HELMORE (*embarrassed*). Did I ?

MADAME KLOST. One *pound*.

HELMORE (*hastily and apologetically*). I hadn't got ten shillings.

MADAME KLOST (*simply*). It was so much to me. I was so poor. My husband was now dead and I could make no money, because I could not walk to look for work. But since I had your fortune, I could go to my Legation to pray them to help me and my little children.

(*Play this scene for a big laugh.* HELMORE *in vain trying to quiet her volubility. The doctors nearly desperate and deafened.* MADAME KLOST *getting more and more rapid and emphatic till: " Always in my prayers, etc." ; which should be played and heard quietly.*)

And there they told me of the wonderful Ragatzy and sent me to him with a letter. Ah, sir, without that money, figure to yourself, it would not have been possible I should have gone. Always in my prayers I say to God I do not know your name, but that I know *He* knows it.

HELMORE (*embarrassed*). Do you really think so? (*About to move up stage.* TOLLEMACHE *stops him.*)

TOLLEMACHE (*with a whimsical smile*). And so it is you, you young devil, who have brought this on us. . . .

HELMORE (*harassed*). Why do I *do* these things? (*Moves up* C.)

MADAME KLOST. Ah! Mr. Ragatzy is rude and rough, yes, but he has the golden heart. He told me he would treat me without any payment at *all*, if only I would tell the others. . . .

TOLLEMACHE. Hah! Tell the others. . . .

MADAME KLOST. So, to-day I have come to let you see me, . . . See . . . I walk for you again? . . . (*Parades across stage with proud satisfaction.*)

TOLLEMACHE. It's marvellous.

MADAME KLOST (*turning when down* L. *Fervently*). It is a miracle.

HELMORE (*gloomily*). That's the worst of it. *move above table on this line*

(*There comes a thumping knock at the door,* R.U.E. NATHAN *rises, drops* C.R. TOLLEMACHE *rises, stands* R. HELMORE *moves above table.* LADD *stands facing door.*)

LADD. That's Ragatzy. (*Goes to door.*)

TOLLEMACHE. Confound the fellow, does he always knock like the crack of doom! . . .

LADD. Come in, Mr. Ragatzy. Come in.

(*He opens the door and* RAGATZY *appears. A man about 40, sufficiently good-looking, of middle height, with a big, clever-looking head and a jutting chin which he holds thrust forward, and a head of upstanding, black untidy hair rising from broad shoulders. His eyes dart right and left and are at once bold and thoughtful, his manner is aggressive, but nervous in spite of his air of blustering assurance. But though he looks what we call foreign and artistic, his whole dress, linen and person is as scrupuously clean as the exigencies of his profession demand. And his strong, supple, beautiful hands are exquisitely kept and tended. His enormous vitality and supreme self-confidence are a challenge.*)

(*The doctors stiffen instinctively.*)

RAGATZY (*effusively in doorway*). Aha, Mr. Ladd . . . how-do-you-do? Aha, so Madame Klost is here . . . Madame Klost, Madame Klost, Madame Klost. . . . Has she been telling you I am a genius? (*Smiles brilliantly upon them all.*)

HELMORE (*stiffly*). We have been hearing what you have done for her.

RAGATZY (*satisfied*). Not bad, hey?

TOLLEMACHE (*aside*). Bounder.

RAGATZY (*goes to door* R.U.E. *and re-enters, dragging after him what looks like a light steel stretcher mounted on four bicycle wheels, which he slews round and runs lightly* L.C.). And here also is my Rack to speak for himself and me. (*To* LADD.) If you will introduce us to these gentlemen.

LADD (*mechanically*). Sir Montague Tollemache . . . Mr. Ragatzy, Sir Nathan Israel, Mr. Vincent Helmore.

(RAGATZY *bows respectfully, deeply to the titles, nods briefly to* HELMORE.)

RAGATZY (*looking round*). But where is the ger-reat Mr. Sturdee ? I come here to catch the big fish . . . not the small fry. . . .

TOLLEMACHE. *Good* Lord !

(NATHAN *calms* TOLLEMACHE *and sits* ~~before~~ *above* *table*.)

LADD. Mr. Sturdee has just left. He has to go to Newcastle for a big operation to-morrow morning.

RAGATZY. Has he, indeed ! I also go to Newcastle for *my* operations. The little Lady Cynthia *Tyne* is my patient.

(HELMORE *sits top of table*.)

So I know there is no train till two-thirty. . . . Why then does he leave from here so early when he knows that I am coming ? He will not meet me, hey ?

LADD (*nervously*). Er—no.

RAGATZY. Why not ?

TOLLEMACHE (*very impressively*). He has seen Captain Wycherly. (*Snorts. Sits* R. *of table*.)

RAGATZY. Ach, that young man, he is my hoodoo ! Why did I let him melt my heart like butter with his tale he has no brains so he must have two legs to work on his farm in Africa or starve.

(MADAME KLOST *is motioned into chair down* L. *by* LADD.)

And so I try, at his own risk, and succeed very nearly. But I fail. *Just* like a doctor. So Mr. Sturdee will not meet me. But you will. Why *is* that ? If you will meet me, why not he ?

HELMORE. Mr. Ragatzy, I think we had better tell you in confidence he has a very painful tragedy in his family. His only daughter, a very brilliant musician and composer, is a cripple.

RAGATZY (*eagerly incredulous, leaning forward*). He cannot cure her ?

LADD (*gravely*). No. . . . (*Standing with foot on lower bar of Rack*.)

RAGATZY (*with satisfaction*). He is a doctor and he has a daughter that he cannot cure ! That puts him in a stupid situation. (*Sits on Rack preparing to confront them all*.)

B

HELMORE.   An intensely painful one.

RAGATZY (*softly*).   He does not like it.   Hey ?   And he would like it still less if I were to cure her . . . Klost also was a cripple . . . and you have seen her . . . ah, it was like the Bible, she lay down upon the Rack and she rose up and walked. . . .   In three months more she will not even limp.   Now, why should it not be the same with this Sturdee girl ?   (*Rises in challenge.*)

TOLLEMACHE (*grimly—rising*).   Mr. Ragatzy, *possibly* you will understand the reason why Miss Sturdee will not be sent to you, when I tell you that her incurable condition is due to the mischief done by an unqualified practitioner when she was a child.

RAGATZY (*his face falling woefully*).   A . . . oh . . . and . . . so he calls out against us all.   *Well*, but he might change his tune if an unqualified practitioner were to cure her now she is grown up. . . . She makes music, does she ?   Is she a celebrity ?   That is always a good advertisement.

(NATHAN *faces* TOLLEMACHE *across the table.*)

TOLLEMACHE (*sotto voce*).   God help me to bear this man !

RAGATZY (*with a sudden brain wave*).   Aha, I know her. . . . Yes. . . .   She is the *Lalage* Sturdee who wrote the music version of the " School for Scandal," is she not ?

HELMORE.   She is.

RAGATZY.   Ah, but her music is charming . . . delicious.   That aria in Act I of Lady Teasle's . . . (*sings*)—" Sir Peter, Sir Peter, I vow I never met . . ."   (*Executes a dance step, holding out the skirts of his coat as for a curtsy.*)

TOLLEMACHE.   Mountebank !   (*Snorts.*)

RAGATZY.   But . . . is she not as pretty as her music ? . . . But . . . to compose like that must be delight !   but—*does it console her for being a cripple ?*

ISRAEL.   It does not console her father.

RAGATZY.   For not being able to cure her.   And he is a master of surgery.   That is how much good his degree does for *him* and for her—Is he *afraid* to meet me ?   Afraid that I might make her well ?

TOLLEMACHE.   Or worse.

RAGATZY.   He thinks *that*, does he ?   And so he will not let me see her.   Very well, if she were my daughter she should not see *him*.

(*Sensation.*)

ISRAEL (*quietly emphatic, dismissing his impudence and recalling him to business*).   Mr. Ragatzy, we are here to examine your *Rack*. From what we have seen of Madame Klost, and heard from Mr. Ladd of the cases you have treated under him . . .

RAGATZY (*insolently*).   Over him. . .!

(NATHAN rises, quietens TOLLEMACHE *and stands behind him.*)

(*His manner changing swiftly to eagerness and earnestness.*) So you will examine my Rack . . . you will fall in love with him . . . he is so beautiful. . . . There! There! There! Turn that bolt please, Mr. Ladd.

(NATHAN *and* HELMORE *rise.*)

The whole frame can be lifted off the wheels—(*lifts it*)—like so, and laid upon a bed or couch. See . . . feel the strength. You cannot break it . . . yet it is so light. . . .

HELMORE. By Jove, it is!

ISRAEL. The workmanship is beautiful . . . beautiful.

RAGATZY. Aha! That is because I made it. Look at these. (*Flourishes fingers in front of him.*)

(*N.B.*—RAGATZY'S *hands should be made up very carefully to look very white and long. None of the other men should make up their hands at all, to heighten the contrast.*)

Are they the hands of an artist or an artisan? Now we show the mechanism. (*Replaces frame on wheels.*)

(LADD L. *of head* R. *helps to fit the Rack together again.* TOLLEMACHE *crosses to head of Rack.* HELMORE *to* L. *of Rack.* NATHAN *eventually kneels to look at mechanism at the floor of Rack.*)

The wheel that turns the pulleys is worked by electricity . . . brains . . . you attach it to an ordinary lamp . . . like this. (*He dexterously removes the electric light globe and inserts the attachment on a long silk cord.*) Now switch the light on. . . . Thank you. Now it is going. Look, you cannot see the turning of the wheel, because it pulls only the one thousandth part of an inch an hour. But it is working all the time, you can just feel the vibration.

TOLLEMACHE (*laying his hand upon the frame*). Only just.

RAGATZY. You understand, it takes one thousand hours to pull one inch. Is that not gentle? Has Madame told you that we did not hurt her?

HELMORE. Yes. Very ingenious. Upon my soul! I'd have liked Sturdee to have seen this. (*Rising and pacing backwards, staring at Rack, then turns away to* R.)

RAGATZY (*moving down—snarling*). He would not have *looked* at it.

TOLLEMACHE (*dryly*). On the contrary, Mr. Ragatzy, he was quite prepared to examine your *Rack*.

RAGATZY. Oh, he *was*? Then why did he not stay? . . . Hey? . . . Why not?

(HELMORE *crosses down* R.)

Why not?

(TOLLEMACHE *crosses* R. *to chair.*)

Why not ?   (*He crosses to above Rack.*) *below*,

(NATHAN *crosses* R. ~~*above*~~ *table.*)

(RAGATZY *stands at bay at* . . . *the final " Why not ? " directed straight at* TOLLEMACHE, *who snorts indignantly as he moves away.*)

LADD (*murmurs*).   Wait a minute . . . wait a minute.

(*The other three doctors rise and walk judicially back to the fireplace, talking in low tones as they go.*)

RAGATZY (*still more insistent*).   Hey ? . . .

HELMORE.   Will you tell him, Tolly ?

TOLLEMACHE.   No . . . I shall lose my temper.   (*Sits in revolving chair* R. *of table, turning his back to* RAGATZY.)

HELMORE (*to* ISRAEL).   You ?

ISRAEL (*disclaiming gracefully*).   I would rather *you* !

HELMORE.   Very well.   (~~*Below table in front of chair above door.*~~) Mr. Ragatzy, we agree you have the right to ask that question— though I think you know the answer—but we wish you to hear it from us officially, as a matter of courtesy . . .

RAGATZY (*snarlingly sarcastic*).   Ah ! . . .   (*Ironical gesture with hands and shoulders.*)

HELMORE.   —And justice.   I may say that I and my colleagues are entirely satisfied that your Rack is the most wonderful . . . beautifully made thing of its kind.

RAGATZY.   He has not a kind.   He is unique.

HELMORE.   Yes, I will even go so far as to agree with you and say that I should like to send some of my patients to you.

TOLLEMACHE (*sotto voce*).   Send him patients ! . . .   (*Snorts.*)

ISRAEL.   I also.

TOLLEMACHE (*grudgingly*).   You too ! . . .   Oh ! . . .

HELMORE.   And I should be willing to work—(*swallowing his gorge*)—*with* you . . . if . . .

RAGATZY (*dragging the words out*).   If . . . if . . . if . . . if . . . if . . .

HELMORE.   There are first of all one or two points on which we shall require to be satisfied.

RAGATZY.   What are they ?   What are they ?

NATHAN.   First of all as regards money—your prices in fact.

RAGATZY.   *Fees !* . . .

TOLLEMACHE (*swinging round in chair*).   We have heard of your charging sometimes seventy pounds, sometimes a hundred and twenty and on one occasion *two hundred and fifty* for your Rack.

RAGATZY (*nodding*).   According to what they can pay.   You charge some people less : I charge some people more.   Only I tell them about it . . . you don't.

TOLLEMACHE.   Mr. Ragatzy, *we* consider there should be only one price for a surgical instrument.

RAGATZY (*sitting astride chair, with its back to them* L. *of table*).
Mr. Surgeons, I consider there should only be two prices . . .
nothing and too much. Those that cannot pay enough . . . pay
nothing . . . and those that can, pay double.

TOLLEMACHE. Infamous.

RAGATZY (*rises and puts back chair by table*). *Famous.* I say to
Lord Tyne : "I will not come to Newcastle for one operation.
The little Lady Cynthia, very uninteresting. A three-year-old
baby, Pooh ! Harley Street can cure her !" But there is a case in
Newcastle Infirmary, a poor boy of twenty . . . very difficult . . .
very complicated . . . I say to Lord Tyne, "Pay me . . . two
fifty and I will do him, also your baby, and come up to Newcastle
once a month to see them both."

TOLLEMACHE. Bolshevism !

RAGATZY (*smilingly*). Brotherhood ! I make them both quite
well. That is all right, hey ?

TOLLEMACHE. Good God ! Do you imagine that we are going
to send you our patients to be plundered for your paupers ?

RAGATZY. I don't want to plunder anyone. Listen, you want
one price for one thing, very well . . . I charge them all two hundred fifty. . . . Honour is satisfied, also Ragatzy. Is that all the
points you want to stick into me ? (*Sits on Rack.*)

(*Pause.*)

HELMORE. No, it is not.

RAGATZY. Well ?

HELMORE. There is the matter of your qualifications. You
have no degree, I think.

RAGATZY. I *have* a degree.

HELMORE (*contemptuously*). What ?

RAGATZY (*coolly*). Of proficiency. . . . Look at her !—(*points
to* MADAME KLOST)—*and here !*—(*points to Rack and slaps his hand
upon it*).

TOLLEMACHE. Have you a degree of *medicine* ?

RAGATZY (*jocularly*). M.D. . . . hey ? What does that mean ?
Mentally Deficient. (*Up C. to* NATHAN.)

(TOLLEMACHE *moves to door and is checked by* HELMORE *and moves
up stage to window.*)

ISRAEL (*gravely*). Mr. Ragatzy, you will gain nothing by flippancy
. . . or insult.

RAGATZY. No, no. (*Spreads hands penitently.*) But I am
sorry . . . very sorry. . . . Ah, I have a wicked tongue. Why
do you not bite the tip off for me, Madame Klost, hey ? (*Turning and speaking confidentially and urgently.*) Look, you want me
to have letters after my name, yes. That satisfies you and satisfies
the public. Then *give* them to me.

TOLLEMACHE (*standing* R. *of table*). Are you *suggesting* that we should recommend the Royal College of Surgeons to confer an honorary degree on you ?

RAGATZY (*coolly*). Why not ?

TOLLEMACHE. Deceive the public ! Pretend that we are satisfied you have sufficient knowledge of surgery to practise.

(RAGATZY *moves up* L. *and returns* C. *on next line.*)

HELMORE. Have you ever walked a hospital, or studied anatomy except from a book ?

RAGATZY (*gratingly*). Yes.

TOLLEMACHE. Where, may I ask ?

RAGATZY (L.C.—*harshly*). Where, may you ask ? In the stock-yards at Chicago. *The slaughter house.*

TOLLEMACHE (*aghast*). Good . . . God. (*Collapses in chair* R. *of table.*)

RAGATZY. Where was I, a poor boy, to get blood and bones . . . ? Ach, many times I have been soaked in scarlet.

HELMORE. Then . . . are we to understand that you began as a butcher ?

RAGATZY. Butcher . . . no. I began as apprentice to my uncle, he made splints for doctors. Bah, they come to us and tell us we must make instruments that are mechanical impossibilities . . . so we despair, we make bad instruments or not at all, because we do not know anatomy to translate into good mechanics. So I say : " My uncle, release me for one year . . . I go and cut up carcasses to find out how the joints fit in the sockets, what hold them and what makes them bend, and then we will make the finest instruments in all the world."

HELMORE (*drawing a long breath*). Well. . . .

TOLLEMACHE. Upon my word !

ISRAEL. That accounts, then, for your extraordinary practical knowledge.

RAGATZY. Of *course*. But you are shocked, hey ?

HELMORE. Well.

(TOLLEMACHE *snorts vigorously.*)

ISRAEL (*at top of table*). Mr. Ragatzy, we appreciate your energy, your enterprise and your *courage*. And we realize that you cannot be . . . and should not . . . be content to be merely a mechanic working under surgeons. Then why not do the theoretical work also ? Qualify. . . .

RAGATZY. What ? Spend four years, like a little boy, studying books and writing answers to examination papers ! You think I leave my work all that time ? Leave cripple people waiting to be cured. Children . . . so I can learn Greek and Latin names for English bones. . . . NO.

TOLLEMACHE. Then you will understand, if you will not qualify, that *if* I, I say *if* I, and my colleagues are to work with you, you must undertake no case without a surgeon.

RAGATZY. What? *You* forbid *me* to take cases without *you*! Oh, my God in heaven!!!!

TOLLEMACHE. That is our rule.

RAGATZY. Trade Union rules, hey? . . . To prevent the unemployment among surgeons.

TOLLEMACHE (*unmoved*). To protect the public from unqualified practitioners.

RAGATZY (*faces the doctors*). Then you would protect them even from the Christ. . . . Ach, if He did His miracles before your noses, you would make it law that He must no more raise the dead unless there is a doctor present, to protect the corpse.

TOLLEMACHE (*rising quietly*). Mr. Ragatzy, when you can raise the dead . . . we will discuss the matter with you. . . . *Till* then . . .

(NATHAN *moves and checks* TOLLEMACHE. RAGATZY *moves up* C.)

RAGATZY (L.C. *down stage, snarling*). Well . . . till then. . . . What? . . .

ISRAEL (*takes a step to* R. *of table*). That is for you to say. We have stated our ultimatum . . . and now await yours. . . .

RAGATZY (*at bay*). So you will not tell your college to give me degree for surgeon . . . ?

ISRAEL. They would not give it if we did.

TOLLEMACHE (*crosses to* RAGATZY, C., *and getting* L. *of him slightly above*). *No.* They have refused it to better men than you, sir, men of honour and good standing, worth and decency, who have wanted to be let in by the back door. But there is no back door to the Royal College of Surgeons—and no lift. Those who wish to enter must climb up by the front steps.

(RAGATZY *laughs during this speech, and faces audience.* TOLLE-
MACHE, *utterly disgusted, turns away up* C.)

ISRAEL. Or remain outside. (*In front of and below table.*)

RAGATZY (*in a white heat of anger, towering to his full height*). I will not stay outside. However much you bar me out, I will come in. I break down bars and bolts. I blow a hole in the back wall with high explosives to make a door for me. I set the world on fire to burn your college down. What? . . . they will keep me out when they have let you in! Bah . . . in my country they do not let you live in the same street as me. We shut you up in ghettoes. Make pogroms of you. (*Laughs wildly and moves up stage* L.)

(ISRAEL *stiffens and quivers, his eyes dilate, his face hardens terribly.*)

HELMORE (*laying his hand upon his arm*). For God's sake, Israel, come away!

ISRAEL (*almost voiceless*). Yes . . . I will not answer him.

(*He turns with* HELMORE *towards door* R.)

TOLLEMACHE (*tersely*). Swine. (*Turns down right after the others.*)

RAGATZY (*furiously*). Swine . . . am I ? . . . Very well then, Mr. Swine can root for himself and find out truffles. But you are sheep, who all must go as you are driven. Who all go after one another because you have not the brains to find out which way to go.

(*They begin to go out singly through the door.* LADD *lingers.*)

(*Warning for Curtain.*)

Follow my leader, Mr. Sturdee . . . sheep. Sheep ! *Sheep !* Bah ! Baa-aa-aaa.

(*Exeunt* TOLLEMACHE *last. The door shuts after them, leaving* LADD *standing irresolute.* LADD crosses R.)

Ach, I would like to cut them into joints for Sunday dinner ! (*Turning ferociously to* LADD.) Why did you bring me here for this ? (*Stops* LADD *as he is crossing, front of him.*)

LADD (*with feeling,* R. *of* RAGATZY). I didn't bring you here for this. . . . It's damnable . . . disgraceful. Why, you fool . . . you've done for yourself. Why did you let your tongue go.

RAGATZY. Mr. Sturdee, he went before my tongue. . . . Do you think that I don't know when he has gone out through that door . . . the rest would go through after. Why don't you go through also, you insider ? (*Moves up* L. *towards head of Rack.*)

LADD (*weakly*). I must. (*Moves* R.)

RAGATZY. Yes, you must. Because I've done with you. . . . I take no more your cases . . . you are a doctor and I am against them all . . . I and the little Klost.

LADD. But those we're doing ?

RAGATZY (*coolly, as he detaches the attachment from the electrolier*). They can choose. Either to go on without you or me. I turn you out, my friend . . . like so . . .

(*Switches out light.*)

Good-bye.

LADD (*going out at door*). I'll let them know the sort of man they'll have to deal with. Pack up your things—then clear. . . .

RAGATZY (*nodding*). Cer . . . tainly. . . .

(*Exit* LADD R.) *left.*

(*Warning for Curtain.*)

(*This should be a big stunt for* RAGATZY. *He shakes his fists after* LADD, *grinding his teeth, and shaking his head, standing with one foot on chair* L. *of table, his elbow on his knee, his chin on hand. His eyes flash, his mind works busily. At last he gives a shout of triumph, turns up stage exultantly, then returns to Rack.* RAGATZY *works busily at the Rack, getting it ready for removal. He has suddenly become very cheerful and pleased with himself. He hums and twists his mouth into a sardonic smile.*)

MADAME KLOST (*advancing timidly*). Can I please go now? I have been so long.

RAGATZY (*grimly*). No . . . you cannot go. Sit down. I want you. (*Grimly slow and hypnotic.*) Madame Klost . . . Madame Klost . . . Madame Klost . . . (*His voice gets more and more threatening with each dragging repetition of her name.*)

MADAME KLOST (*sits down* L. *again*). You want me. . . . For what more than this?

RAGATZY. Do you think that you have paid me by this morning's work? Bah! Did you persuade the doctors to give me a degree? Did you support me. . . . Did you defend me? . . . Did you turn on them like a fury, when I was attacked . . . or did you sit there mum as a mild mouse? Hey?

MADAME KLOST (*distressed*). Sir, how could I speak against all these grand doctor gentlemen—(RAGATZY *laughs and repeats* "GRAND *Gentlemen*") . . . when you speak *all* the time and make them angry?

RAGATZY (*indulgently*). Perhaps . . . the little Klost has reason. Perhaps she has. . . . So she shall have another chance to pay before I take away my Rack and give her no more treatment. . . .

MADAME KLOST (*almost voiceless with horror*). Take it away from me!

RAGATZY. It is not yours. You have not paid for it.

MADAME KLOST. But you have told me, if I do not lie all night upon it three more months . . .

RAGATZY (*nodding*). You will again be cripple. Do you like to see your children starve . . . because you cannot go to work? Then you must pay me by finding patients rich enough to pay for both.

MADAME KLOST. How can I? All those I know of cripples are more poor than I. I told you then, I tell you now again, I know no rich people.

RAGATZY (*slowly watching her very closely*). You know of one rich woman who is lame.

MADAME KLOST. I do? I do *not*. What one is this?

RAGATZY. Miss Sturdee. Lalage Sturdee.

MADAME KLOST. Miss Lalage Sturdee.

RAGATZY. You heard them talk of her.

MADAME KLOST. Yes. But to hear of her is not to know her.

RAGATZY. You can make her acquaintance.

MADAME KLOST. I ?

RAGATZY. Yes . . . you.

MADAME KLOST. *Oh !* . . . oh ! What do you *mean* ?

RAGATZY (*impressively*). I mean to cure her.

MADAME KLOST. Oh !

RAGATZY. That will make them recognize me. Make them sit up, hey ? But she first must hear of me. And know what I have done . . . from *you*.

MADAME KLOST. *From me ?* (*Stares at him frightened, but held by his spell.*)

RAGATZY. Yes, you. Always you. To-morrow, before her father is returned, call at her house. . . .

MADAME KLOST. At her house ?

RAGATZY. In Harley Street !

MADAME KLOST. But she will not see me !

RAGATZY. You must make her. Send in messages until she does. If not . . .

MADAME KLOST (*terrified*). You will take away the Rack ? . . .

RAGATZY. *Yes*, unless you make Miss Sturdee promise she will see me. Listen, I shall be waiting there outside. You tell her that. Tell her the doctors will not let her see me because they are *afraid* . . . that I will cure her. Tell her the truth . . . I am an outsider . . . I am . . . a swine. But I *do* cure people !

(*He stands over her fascinating her with his mesmerism : her frightened, wide eyes, fixed on him.*)

CURTAIN.

To face page 27]

ACT II

SCENE.—LALAGE'S *music-room, Harley Street.*

TIME.—*The afternoon of the following day.*

A very pleasant room, slightly futurist, a few choice pieces of furniture only and one good picture on the brightly coloured walls . . . the whole room expresses the personality of one who has beautifully rebelled against convention. There is an Oriental day-bed by the fire R. and a grand piano down stage L. where LALAGE *sits leisurely correcting a score and occasionally striking a note or trying a phrase. She wears an artistic but fashionable delicate-coloured tea-frock harmonizing with the colour scheme of the room.*

    So long as she is seated there is nothing to betray the fact that she is a cripple. Her back is perfectly straight and supple, her bust and shoulders beautifully formed. But among the sheets of manuscript music which lie scattered to her right on the floor, lies her invalid's stick with an india-rubber ferrule.

    Door L.C. *Tall Georgian window and window seat* C.)

(Enter PRITCHARD, *a high superior middle aged parlourmaid with a supercilious air, which indicates that she considers herself more Harley Street than all its specialists. She has also a taste for Johnsonian English and the grand manner exhibited by stage Duchesses.)*

PRITCHARD (*at door*). Miss Lalage . . . (*Gives an apologetic cough* C.)

LALAGE (*impatiently, without looking up*). Pritchard, I told you I was not to be disturbed. I'm working—at least, I'm trying to work.

PRITCHARD (*coming* L.C. *to* R. *of chair*). I am aware you said so, miss. There *was* a person wanting to see you, a woman, I *suppose* you'd call her.

LALAGE. Who was she?

PRITCHARD. She said something about clo'es, miss, and thinking it was old clo'es she meant, I said you hadn't none to sell and she must go away.

LALAGE (*looking up*). Well!

PRITCHARD. Well, miss, she wouldn't go nor yet say what she wanted, so I shut the door on her.

27

LALAGE. Quite right, Pritchard, I can't see people who won't say what they want. Can I ?

PRITCHARD. They always want money, miss.

LALAGE. What are you waiting for ? (*Pause.*)

PRITCHARD (*impressively*). Mr. Basil Owen has called.

LALAGE (*arrested*). Oh . . . *has* he !

PRITCHARD. Yes, miss. I thought you'd see *him*. So I let him in at once, because that woman was still hanging about.

LALAGE (*half apologetically*). Well . . . I really am waiting for him.

PRITCHARD (*with an absolutely expressionless face and voice that are somehow full of meaning*). Yes, miss . . . I'll tell him. (*Exit* L.)

(LALAGE *looks after her with a half-amused, half-rueful expression. She plays passionate sweeping strings of joyous music.*)

(*Enter* BASIL, *young, good-looking, light-footed and delightful. One sees the reflection of his radiance, as well as an inner radiance of her own illumined in* LALAGE'S *eyes and face.*)

BASIL (*crossing to piano*). Oh, Lally darling. (*Kisses her hand.*) I told the superior Miss Pritchard she needn't show *me* up. I'm terrified of her. She always looks at me as though she thought no one without at least two broken legs and a Rolls-Royce ought to expect *her* to open the door to them.

LALAGE (*stretching her hand out and rallying him tenderly*). Were you sure you knew the way ? You haven't been here for so long.

BASIL (*below piano in loop—a little constrained, leaning over the piano*). No, I haven't, have I ? Well, how are you, bless you. . . . How's the great work ?

LALAGE. It isn't working.

BASIL. Oh !

LALAGE. At least it wasn't till you came.

BASIL. Ah !

LALAGE. I do believe I've got the joy note I want for the leit-motiv. Listen. . . . (*Plays a triumphant phrase.*)

BASIL (*always in loop of piano*). Oh, top *hole* . . . top hole.

LALAGE. What I want now is some more libretto. Have you done any ?

BASIL (*shaking head before speaking*). No, my dear, stuck entirely. (*Crosses* R., *then up* C.) Been sitting in front of my paper chewing my penholder for a week. And now I've come round to see you to be re-inspired.

LALAGE (*gently reproachful*). Why did you wait ?

BASIL. My dear, I've been so full up. Dancing every night *and* in the afternoon most days. And now there's tennis, I don't think I ever *shall* do any work. I must though. Tell me I must . . .

~~Lally.~~ Talk to me and make me want to. I do really, only there isn't time because of all the other things. (*Down again level to* LALLY.)

LALAGE (*enviously*). Basil, it must be so perfectly lovely to be like that. I can't scold you, though I ought to. But I'm not feeling virtuous. Let's go and sit over there and tell each other things. (*She begins to gather up music.*)

BASIL (*crosses to piano*). Ra-ther. I'll get these for you. (*Below piano. Stoops and gathers up the sheets which are out of her reach as she sits on the music-stool.*)

LALAGE. I'd have ordered tea early if I'd known you were coming. But father isn't back from Newcastle yet, so I said I'd wait.

(*She rises, leaning her hand on the piano, and balances herself carefully before she takes a step. One sees the tragedy of her life in every movement, as resting first one hand and then the other on the piano and leaning nearly all her weight on it, she limps to the end of it, but her stick is still just out of her reach. She frowns a little, as with a quick contraction of pain she realizes her impotence.*)

LALAGE (*to* BASIL). Give me my stick, there's an angel!

BASIL. *Here* you are. (*Rises, puts armful of music on stool, gives stick to her right hand. Waits till she has walked two steps, then behind her to left arm.*) Let me give you an arm. (*Slips his right arm, with deft and practised tenderness, under her left arm and supports her.*)

LALAGE (*blissfully*). Oh, Basil, that *is* a luxury, not a necessity. I didn't know I was tired, but I am.

(BASIL *gets cushion from chair.*)

(*She sinks on to the couch among the cushions and leans her stick against the head to be ready at her right hand.*)

BASIL. Let me put your feet up for you.

LALAGE. No thanks, not now.

BASIL. Well then, lie back and really rest.

(*Lifts them tenderly by the ankles and swings them on to couch.*)

(*Arranging cushions at head of couch.*) Then you'll start going like a two-year-old when you get up. (*Sitting on her left.*)

(*She moves to right by pressing her arms on couch and making her right thigh drag her whole body. The movement is so quickly and deftly done, one hardly notices that the left limb is almost powerless and does none of the work of lifting, but has only the strength enough to draw itself after the rest of the body.*)

(BASIL *settles himself in a comfortable lolling position by her feet, and lights a cigarette as she continues dreamily.*)

LALAGE. Sometimes, I *do* feel as though I weren't limping at all. When I'm working and my head's full of the most heavenly music, I'm simply not conscious of it. It's just as though I'm upheld by beautiful dream pinions and I go sailing along until some brute of a tender-hearted woman says . . . " How *dreadful* it is to see you so lame."

BASIL (*incredulously*). They don't ? Not really ! !

LALAGE (*with energy*). They *do*, Basil. Why don't they teach the women of our class decency. They come up to me . . . in hotels and places . . . perfect strangers, and ask me what's the matter with me, and . . . and *have* I been to anyone about it !

BASIL. I know : Thank God men don't do that sort of thing.

LALAGE. No. In all my life, I've never known a man, or a poor person, man or woman, do anything that wasn't most beautifully tactful.

BASIL (*taking hand*). Have *I* never hurt you, Lally ?

LALAGE. Never, ~~never~~, never . . . that *way*. I don't mind your talking about it because you do it naturally and never when anybody's there. I don't ~~ever~~ mind your knowing how much I mind. I can't ever talk to father about that. It would seem like reproaching him.

BASIL (*with understanding*). Yes . . . of course.

LALAGE. So it's good for me to get it off my chest to you sometimes, how I ~~do~~ want to murder every one that pities me . . . ~~and~~ damn the eyes of every one that stares. (*Penitently.*) Forgive me, old thing, I'm not often like this, am I ? But when I can't work . . . and forget . . .

BASIL. Lally, you couldn't work because I kept you waiting, brute that I am.

LALAGE (*her tender radiance returning*). Never mind, my dear, you've come now.

BASIL (*ruefully*): But I've brought you nothing. (*Rises and crosses to piano.*)

LALAGE. You've brought yourself. (*Quietly.*) That's all I want. When you come, the music comes . . . melodies . . . harmonies, orchestration . . . everything. Basil ? . . .

BASIL. Yes ? . . .

LALAGE. Do you know sometimes I've been stuck for days over a beastly technical thing like consecutive fifths, then I just get a whiff of that stuff you put on your hair . . . (*They both laugh.* BASIL *back by then, standing by chair left of her*)—and those fifths un-consecutive themselves all by their little lones. I laugh, it's so ridiculous. But . . . (*to herself*)—it's so sweet——

BASIL. Oh, Lally, if you could only *do* things with me ! (*Rises and walks about the room.*) Dance and go topping long walks . . . over the moors for miles and miles. You've never been right in the middle of a moor, deep among the gorse bushes when they're in bloom, smelling of honey and heaven. I'm going to take the girl I love there, one day, and ask her. She couldn't say " No " with all the winds in the world blowing that sweetness to her. Then kiss her under the big open blue.

LALAGE (*in a low strained voice*). Have you met her ?

BASIL. Not yet. Though I often think I have. At dances, when I get a perfect partner, swaying in time to the music with her, feeling absolutely one. Oh, Lally ! when you hold a girl on your heart, she goes to your head. And it's the wine of life.

LALAGE (*steadily*). I've never tasted it.

BASIL (*coming to her right hand*). Lally ! I wish I could give it to you. I *wish* I could.

(*He holds her hand. She presses it limply and then lets it go. He paces about with his back to her, pursuing his own thoughts.*)

BASIL. You see, a man *has* to have a wife who can run about with him and play Games, if he's going to keep out of mischief. Otherwise he's bound to run off the rails running after some one else. Because, you see . . .

LALAGE (*slowly*). He cannot play alone.

BASIL. No. Not if he's like me, the rotten sort that *can't*. *You* know that, Lally, you're such an absolutely understanding pal. *She's* got to be that too, of course. . . . My aunt ! I don't want much, do I ? Shall I ever get it ? Ever find her ?

LALAGE (*with a sigh*). She'll find you. There are about two million of her looking.

BASIL. But there's only *one* . . . one . . . I'll look at. Then, you shall be the first to hear. . . . The very first. . . .

LALAGE (*quietly*). Thank you, dear.

(*There is something in her tone that makes him look at her, but her eyes are averted and a rather constrained silence falls between them. Both look up decidedly relieved as* PRITCHARD *rather abruptly enters the room. She struggles to preserve her superior calm, but she is agitated, indignant and even apologetic.*)

PRITCHARD (C.—*rather breathless*). Miss Lalage, it's that woman again.

LALAGE (*rousing herself*). What woman ? Oh, the one who wasn't Old Clothes and wouldn't say what she wanted. Has she come back ?

PRITCHARD. Yes, miss, and rang again. I could see it was her through the glass, so at first I wouldn't answer, but she kep' on ring, ring, ring, enough to disturb the . . . *whole* . . . house. So I opened the door and asked her *please* to give me a message and I'd take it up to you. Then she started going on most foreign, wringing her hands and saying she only wanted to see you for your own good.

BASIL. Sounds disinterested. *interesting*

PRITCHARD (*impressively*). And that all your life you'd be sorry
if you didn't see her.

LALAGE. Did you say she was foreign ?

PRITCHARD. Yes, miss, very. And so was the man.

BASIL (*interested*). Had she a man with her ?

PRITCHARD. No, sir. Just passing. (*Indicating window.*) But
he stopped and gave me *such* a look. (*Imitating* RAGATZY'S *voice
and manner.*) " You let her in," he says. " You let her in." It
give me quite a turn, for he'd got eyes that went through me like
brad-awls. But before I could give him a sharp answer, he was
down the street.

(LALLY *gets crutch to move up to window*. PRITCHARD *moves up with
her on* LALLY'S R.)

And the woman was in the 'all, 'aving slipped by me. So what was
I to do, miss, but shut the door ?

(BASIL *drops down* R. *to hearthrug.*)

LALAGE. What's she doing now ?

PRITCHARD. Sitting down by the table, crying all over the
appointment book. I said to 'er sharp I did, " My good woman, you
mustn't cry *here*. It's not *your* 'all. Try to behave more English."

LALAGE (C.). Well, we must do something with her. (*Drops to
chair* L. *of bed. Frowning in thought.*) She sounds so damp. . . .

(*The handle of the door is turned furtively from without and the door
pushed half open, showing* MADAME KLOST'S *hand and sleeve.*)

BASIL (*staring*). Hul-*lo* !

(*Enter* MADAME KLOST, *quivering and desperate, but tearless and
determined as though impelled by some unseen force, her handkerchief
crushed tightly in her nervous hand. She comes down stage, walking
as though stiff with terror, between chair and piano,* LALAGE *just
below her.*)

PRITCHARD (*snorting*). The brazen creature ! (*Moving to* MADAME
KLOST *in fury.*)

MADAME KLOST (*speaking mechanically but with intensity*). Mees,
will you not see me ? For your good, for your own great good ?
(*She stands shaken with dry sobs.*)

LALAGE (*aloud*). Please don't distress yourself so, Madame . . .
Close . . . is it ?

MADAME KLOST (*speaking more naturally*). K-lost-t-t, mees.

LAGAGE (*gently*). I'm sure you think there's something very
urgent that you ought to tell me. Won't you sit down ?

(PRITCHARD *takes a step towards* MADAME KLOST.)

MADAME KLOST (*relieved*). Yes, yes. (*Sits.*)

(LALLY *moves down to* MADAME KLOST. MADAME KLOST *sits upright and tense on edge of chair.*)

LALAGE (C., *firmly*). You can go, Pritchard.

PRITCHARD. Miss Lally, it's encouraging Bolsheviks, I call it.

(BASIL *above chair,* L. *of bed.*)

(*Exit* PRITCHARD.)

LALAGE. Now won't you try to tell me quietly what it is ? Then I can see whether there's anything that I can do to help you.

MADAME KLOST (*distressed*). Mees, do you think I want to *beg* of you ?

LALAGE (*guardedly*). You seem . . . in great distress.

MADAME KLOST (*with energy*). No, no! I ask no money. I shall not want it, if you will see *him*.

BASIL (*with distance and suspicion—suddenly*). Him ? . . . Do you mean the man in the street ?

MADAME KLOST. Ah—yes.

LALAGE. *Really!* And who is he ?

MADAME KLOST (*with great simplicity*). Mees, he is Ragatzy.

LALAGE. *RAGATZY ?* I've never heard of him.

BASIL (*thinking*). It's a name I've read in the papers.

LALAGE (*drawing herself up as though scenting battle*). What does he want with me ? (*She moves a limping step.*)

MADAME KLOST (*desperately*). Mees . . . you are so lame !

LALAGE (*astounded. She is speechless.*)

MADAME KLOST (*almost wailing.*) He wants to cure you !

(*With a set face* LALAGE *turns* L., *limps to the sofa, her head turned away from them.*)

BASIL (*eagerly*). Does he think he can ?

MADAME KLOST. Ah . . . yes. (*Rises.*)

LALAGE (*moving away slightly—harshly facing round defensively as though at bay*). *Is* this some New Thought Healing ?

MADAME KLOST. No, *no*.

(BASIL *meets* LALAGE *at foot of sofa.*)

BASIL (*rapidly and tenderly, hanging over her*). Lally, I know now ! It's a man who's got a sort of machine for making people's legs and arms the proper length. I read about it in the " Daily Mercury."

LALAGE (*by foot of bed—coldly*). I don't see the " Daily Mercury." It's rather a rag, isn't it ? (*To* MADAME KLOST.) Is he a doctor ?

MADAME KLOST. No.

LALAGE. I *thought* not. (*Half turns away.*)

BASIL (*breathlessly*). But it says he's done some most marvellous

C

cures. It gives names and addresses. Letters from the people themselves.

MADAME KLOST (*rising, more down* C.). He has cured me. For fifteen years I was more worse than you. I could not go at all without both crutches.

(LALAGE *turns round slowly and looks her up and down.*)

BASIL. Lally, I'd have told you about him, only I thought if he *was* any good, your father would be sure to know.

LALAGE (*scornfully*). Of course.

MADAME KLOST. For Mr. Ladd he has done many cures.

LALAGE (*to* MADAME KLOST, *half arrested*). Ladd! The Cavendish Square man?

MADAME KLOST (C.). Mr. Frederick Ladd. Yes, of Cav-*end*-ish Square.

BASIL (*pressing his advantage*). He's a good man, isn't he?

LALAGE (*coolly*). Pretty good. (*Searchingly to* MADAME KLOST.) Do any of the other surgeons know about this man? Sir Montague Tollemache? (LALLY *moves towards* MADAME KLOST.)

MADAME KLOST (*rapidly*). Mr. Helmore, Sir Nathan Israel, all, all except your father. Mr. Ragatzy brought me to the Hospital only yesterday to show how he has cured me when they could *not.* And only Mr. Sturdee would not wait to see him.

LALAGE (*with triumphant scorn*). Then he didn't think he was worth seeing. (*Moving away from* MADAME KLOST, *sits on foot of couch:*)

MADAME KLOST (*timidly*). No, Mr. Helmore told to Mr. Ragatzy it was because of the great hurt that one bad ignorant has done to you.

LALAGE (*drawing a long breath as though struck with a sudden notion*). Oh . . . was *that* how he came to hear about me?

MADAME KLOST. That makes him want to help you. He says that, even though the doctors have insult him . . . he will be kind to you. He will not leave you in your suffering. He asks that you shall see him now. He waits out in the street. For when he has seen you he will know for sure if he can cure you.

LALAGE (*sharply*). What? (*Aghast at this audacity.*) Do you mean to say that he thinks that I . . . (*With the aid of her hands pressed on the couch she rises to her feet—rising* C. *to face* MADAME KLOST.)

BASIL (*moves forward—*LALLY *puts her hand on his arm to check him*). Oh, Lally! If he *could*!

LALAGE (*putting him away from her*). Basil, Basil, he can't, dear. No one can. I've seen every one. *Every one.*

BASIL. But not this man. (*Urgently.*) Lally, *let* him look at you.

LALAGE (*magnificently*). What! A man like that! A man out

of the street. (*Aside to* Basil.) Basil! . . . And without consulting father.

Madame Klost (*moving up to* Lally). Mr. Ragatzy says that if you wait to ask your father he will never let you see him.

Basil. I don't suppose he will.

Madame Klost. For fear that he should cure you.

Basil. Doctors are like that, aren't they?

Lalage (*flaming proudly*). No! And you don't know my father. Afraid that anyone should cure me! Why, if anyone could . . . he wouldn't care *who* it was. He'd give him thousands. Tell Mr. Ragatzy *that*! (*Eyes fixed on* Madame Klost.)

Madame Klost (*anxiously*). But you will not see him now . . . yourself?

Lalage (*with a curling lip*). Certainly not. (*Turns* R. *towards couch.*) Basil, please ring the bell for Pritchard.

(Basil *goes reluctantly to the bell and rings it.* Madame Klost *rises and, turning blindly towards the door, breaks down and weeps. Sits on piano stool.*)

(*Sitting on bed, wearily impatient.*) Oh, please don't cry. It can't matter to you whether I'm cured or not. It was very good of you to come, but . . .

(Madame Klost *goes on sobbing.* Basil *stands before her sympathetically.*)

Basil (L. *of piano—anxiously*). I say . . . will he be angry with you if Miss Sturdee doesn't see him?

Madame Klost (*sobbing*). Yes . . . yes . . . yes.

Basil (*anxiously*). What will he do?

Madame Klost (*crosses to* Lally—*imploringly*). Mees, I ask you, to see him! See him! Only see him for the sake of me. (*Kneeling.*)

Lalage. Is he going to pay you money if I do? (*New aspect for* Lally.)

Madame Klost. No, no!

Lalage (*sternly*). That's not true. He *is* going to pay you. You *said* you wouldn't want money if I saw him.

Madame Klost. No, no . . . because . . . see here.

(*Movement from* Basil, *trying to raise* Madame Klost. *Holds out a paper piteously, which* Basil *takes. He walks with it to* Lalage, *who takes it from him and reads.*)

Lalage. "To Madame Klost. I, Anton Ragatzy, guarantee to leave my special apparatus, the extension Rack, in your possession and give you all the further treatment that you need if . . ." Oh! . . .

Madame Klost. Mees, he will sign it if I make you see him.

Only to see him, not to let him cure you. Just to see him. He asks nothing more.

LALAGE (*pregnantly*). And if I don't?

MADAME KLOST (*rising slowly*). He takes away the Rack . . . I have to lie on three months more. And I shall go back to a cripple.

LALAGE. Oh! . . . How wicked! . . . How wicked!

BASIL (*pleading—at head of couch*). Lally, you can't let him do that to her? . . .

MADAME KLOST (*with passion*). Mees, you do not know, you don't *know* what it is to be a cripple. (*Turns to* LALAGE.)

LALAGE (*with quiet intensity*). I . . . I don't? . . .

MADAME KLOST (*with a power of pent-up emotion that transfigures her and shakes her fragile frame*). No, no! You are rich! Rich! You need never go when you are tired. You lie in bed . . . on couches: you are carried by your servants: you ride in motors. What does it matter? What does it hurt you to be lame?

(LALAGE *covers her eyes with her hands*.)

You need not work. Do all your housework in your weary pain. And starve because you cannot walk to earn your money for your children's bread . . . see them die of hunger as I shall see my Serge, my Marie, and my little Paul.

LALAGE (*rises*). No. You shan't.

MADAME KLOST (*piteously—back to* LALLY). Oh, I do not want to enter this grand house. I am a coward. It is for them I go into the lion's den.

LALAGE. Oh! You brave poor thing—(*moving to* MADAME KLOST)—don't cry. Don't cry, please! I will see him. (*Embracing her.*)

MADAME KLOST (C.). You will! Yes? (*Moving quickly* C. *Towards door two movements : one by chair, two to door.*)

LALAGE (*terribly*). I will. The utter *cad*!

BASIL (*under his breath*). Oh, good! (*Above* LALLY.)

(*Enter* PRITCHARD. MADAME KLOST *slips furtively out.*)

LALAGE. Pritchard, take Madame Klost downstairs. She's going to fetch the man that spoke to you.

PRITCHARD (*turns to the door and pauses—aghast*). Am I to let him in, miss? A murdering sort of looking man like that! (*By door.*)

LALAGE (*steadily*). Pritchard, I've got to see him. Show him up.

PRITCHARD (*with a flounce*). Well, miss—all I say is it's a good job Mr. Owen's here . . . and a pity the master isn't. (*Exit* PRITCHARD.)

LALAGE. Basil, you will stay?

BASIL (*fervently*). I *will*. He doesn't sound the sort of blighter you ought to see alone.

LALAGE (*furiously*). The arrogance! The insolent arrogance! He's only got to see me, and I'll be persuaded to let him treat me. I haven't any will of my own, or any loyalty to father.

BASIL (*sits* R. *of couch*). Lally, if he *could* cure you! (*Earnestly.*) He does cure poeple. Oh, my dear, if he could, it would be so wonderful! You'd be a woman, not a spirit in prison.

LALAGE (*agonized*). Basil, don't! Don't! Don't! Don't! think of it. Don't make me hope. Father says I mustn't.

BASIL (*his face falling*). Will you tell *him* that?

LALAGE (*with spirit*). I'm not going to tell him anything. . . . Or even let him see me walk . . . I'll just listen quite quietly to what he has to say, then tell him that he's had his pound of flesh, but he shan't touch one single bone.

(*Enter* PRITCHARD. *She flings open the door with a face like a stone wall.*)

PRITCHARD (*moving down*). Miss Lalage—the man . . . (*Words fail her.*)

RAGATZY (*wickedly amiable, as he passes her to* C.). Do not look at me as though you'd like to bite me, if I try to kiss you . . . or I shall not tip you when you show me out.

(PRITCHARD'S *face, as it were, falls to pieces and then builds itself up again as she exits outraged.*)

(MADAME KLOST *waits in doorway till* PRITCHARD *exits.* RAGATZY *drops down to above piano.*)

(*Cheerfully coming down* C. *and looking round about him with genuine admiration.*) What a charming room! You like to get away from Harley Street—hey?

LALAGE (*trenchantly*). And *you* would like to get into it.

RAGATZY (*nodding unembarrassed*). Certainly. And I am here.

LALAGE. Mr. Ragatzy.

RAGATZY (*formally*). Miss Sturdee. Miss Lalage Sturdee.

(*For the first time he looks full at her and lets her look at him straight between the eyes, but he cannot hypnotize her.*)

LALAGE. I understand that you will sign this paper, if I agree to give you an interview.

RAGATZY. Certainly.

LALAGE. Then you shall have one.

RAGATZY. *Twenty* minutes?

LALAGE. I'm glad you think you'll need a little time. Very well then. Twenty minutes. Now please sign. (*Holds out paper.*)

RAGATZY (*taking it from her—puts paper in pocket*). Make the little Klost quite happy, hey? . . . And I let her go.

LALAGE (*coldly pointing up* C.). You'll find pen and ink on that table.

(BASIL *drops up to head of bed.*)

RAGATZY. Over there, hey ? (*Takes paper out of pocket.*) Verree good. Excellent. (*He goes and writes quickly.*)

MADAME KLOST (*to* LALAGE). Mees, how shall I thank you ?
May the good God reward you.

LALAGE (*gently*). Don't worry any more for Serge and Paul and
Marie. They're quite safe.

(*During last two speeches* RAGATZY *gets chair from beside couch and
places it by writing-table up* L. *of window by door* L.C.)

RAGATZY (*grimly jovial—coming to her*). They will be safer if you
witness my signature.

(*Leaves paper on table and comes down* L. *of bed to* LALLY. *As* LALAGE
moves down and up to table, RAGATZY *moves* C. *to watch her.*)

(*Movement from* BASIL *to stop him, which he checks.*)

LALAGE. I will.

(*She limps angrily across the room.* RAGATZY *watches her walk, goes
up to door* C., *stands so that he can look at* LALAGE, *having made a
complete circle of her.*)

(*Signing with an angry dash, rises.*) There ! And if ever he tries
to terrorize you like this again . . .

RAGATZY. Come to you . . . hey ?

LALAGE. Yes.

(RAGATZY *picks up her crutch and hands it to her with a smile. She
takes it angrily and gives paper to* MADAME KLOST.)

MADAME KLOST. Mees, I am so thankful. Thank you.
(*Crossing straight to door.*)

RAGATZY. Run along. (*Pulling notes out of his pocket.*) Here,
buy some candies for the little ones.

MADAME KLOST. Thank you.

RAGATZY. And do not think I am an ogre.

MADAME KLOST. No. (*Exit* MADAME KLOST.)

LALAGE. Aren't you ? (*Moves down by couch.*)

RAGATZY. No. (*Shuts door after* MADAME KLOST, *dropping
down* C.L. *Gradually.*)

LALAGE (*up* C.). But you would have tortured that poor mother !

RAGATZY (*coolly*). Bah ! You think I take away the Rack from
her and spoil my best advertisement ? *No !* Nevaire ! But I
must make her think I *will.* She is a timid little hare who will not
enter in a house like this unless she is frightened to stay outside (L.).
And I must make you think so too, hey ? Mr. Sturdee's daughter
cannot let me in to cure her . . . I am an outsider. But if she
thinks she *must* to save poor Klost . . .

LALAGE. Do you call that honest ?

RAGATZY. Perhaps not. But that should reassure you.

LALAGE. To know that you're not honest ?

RAGATZY (*nodding*). *Cer*-tainly. If I were not genius I should have to be.

BASIL (*half amused*). Oh, I say !

RAGATZY (*by piano*). All is forgiven to celebrities ! (*To* LALAGE.) Your father's daughter could not take a lover. . . . (LALLY *turns to him in sheer amazement.*) But the wonder woman who has made such lovely music can give herself to whom she will and all the world will come more to her Opera.

BASIL. That's true. (*Over by fireplace.*)

RAGATZY. . It is the same with me. Bah ! I am not a doctor who fears to be divorced. I would be very pleased to show you how my patients still would come flocking if my wife divorce me. Unfortunately I have divorce her long ago.

(BASIL *down* R.)

(LALAGE, *angry movement to foot of bed.* RAGATZY *moves* C. *quickly to watch her walk and* LALAGE *sways round. Unfortunately he is unguarded enough to pace away from* LALAGE *at this moment to watch her, so that* LALLY *sees what he is doing.*)

LALAGE. Oh ! What are you doing ? You're looking at me like a doctor. I won't have it. (*Piteously.*) Basil . . . (*Stops and sways.*)

(BASIL *comes quickly to her and puts his arm round her, on* LALLY'S *right side.*)

RAGATZY (*coolly*). Oh it's all right ! I have seen you walk, and when you were not thinking. That is good, hey ?

BASIL (*whispering*). Lally, don't mind.

LALAGE. I *do* mind.

RAGATZY. Never mind. Mr. Owen, take her to the sofa. I will not look. (*Turns away to piano, looks at opera score.*)

(BASIL *leads her to the sofa, and she leans back, beating her angry hands upon the cushions.*)

(*Pause.*)

RAGATZY. You are recovered from the little shock, hey ?

(BASIL *puts crutch under couch and is standing left of bed. Pats cushions for* LALLY, *and* RAGATZY *moves away to left of bed.*)

Not quite ? Then I will sit down and assume a bedside manner to reassure you. (*Gets chair from writing-table, sits well forward with his knees apart.*) Put out your tongue and say ninety-nine.

(BASIL *moves round to* L. *of* RAGATZY. BASIL *chuckles.* LALAGE *stares indignantly, but* RAGATZY *simply puts on a ludicrous imitation of an old-style physician and she bursts into a little shrieking sob of involuntary laughter.)*

LALAGE. Oh, why do I *laugh* ? (*Angry with herself.*)

RAGATZY (*with satisfaction*). Because I make you. I make you let me in. I make you walk. I make you laugh. (*Slowly.*) And . . .

BASIL (*slightly above* LALAGE—*eagerly*). Can you make her well ?

(*Quick breath from* LALAGE.)

RAGATZY (*seriously*). Does she *want* to *be* well ?

BASIL. Of course she does.

RAGATZY (*shaking head*). She does not say so.

(*Rises—leads* BASIL *down to piano—so he can talk to* LALAGE *alone.* BASIL *understands—leans on piano, quietly looking at music.*)

Last night I say to myself: " What is she like, this Lalage ? " (*Back to* LALAGE.) Then I get the score of her so lovely opera and play over on my 'cello veree slow and veree soft, to hear what things her soul is saying.

LALAGE. What did you hear ?

RAGATZY (*sits* L. *of bed—nodding*). That you are not a sofa saint, although you lie upon a sofa. Your music is not hymn tunes. There is the devil in it.

LALAGE. You've got good ears.

RAGATZY. And you have passion. You give your burning love to some one who does not love you. That *makes* for you your music. And for us. *We* like it. You like it, hey ?

LALAGE. Like what ?

RAGATZY (*leaning towards her*). Not to be loved like other women (*Pauses and watches her wince and struggle.*) And tell us so in music. Be-you-ti-ful, heavenly music. But if I cure you so you can marry, you will tell your passion by your kisses in his arms.

LALAGE. How dare you ?

RAGATZY. Bah ! You will be too tired . . . too banale. You become fat mother . . . not great artist. (*Rapidly.*) Yes, you are very wise to not want to be well. (*Rises and walks down stage to* BASIL.) We will talk no more of curing. . . . You shall play me music in the ten minutes I have left. . . . No. No . . . No . . . I will not cure you. She shall stay a cripple. That will please her father. (*Moves up* C.)

LALAGE (*coldly*). That is a *lie* . . . (*sitting up*)—Mr. Ragatzy, I didn't mean . . . to see you.

RAGATZY (*nodding*). I know you didn't mean ! (*Facing* LALAGE.)

LALAGE. But as we have got so far and . . .

RAGATZY. Aha ! We have got so far, have we ? (*Moving towards* LALAGE.)

LALAGE.   You'd better see the X-ray photos of me.   Then you'll know.   And then you'll go.

RAGATZY (*his face falling*).   AH !

BASIL.   Shall I ring for them, Lally ?

LALAGE.   Yes, please.

(BASIL *moves as if to ring bell.*)

No, no.   Tell Miss Cross to give them to you.

(BASIL *moves up towards door.*)

Tell her the big ones that were taken to show Moritz.

RAGATZY.   Ah, you have seen Moritz !   (*Up to bed again.*)   In Vienna.   What did he say ?

LALAGE.   That he could have cured me if I'd been under ten.

RAGATZY.   And you were ?

LALAGE (*steadily*).   Twenty-two.

RAGATZY (*impressively sitting L. of bed and looking at* LALAGE).   I have cured two young men Moritz could not.   Thirty and thirty-three.

BASIL (*excitedly*).   Lally, you're years off that.

(*Long pause before she speaks.*)

LALAGE (*with a quick-drawn breath*).   Fetch the photos.

BASIL.   I *will*.   (*Exit* BASIL.)

(RAGATZY *follows him up*   LALAGE'S *face is strained, her eyes search* RAGATZY'S.)

RAGATZY (*with admiration*).   What a beautiful young man !

LALAGE (*briefly*).   Yes.

RAGATZY (*confidentially, moving slightly down to* C.).   You love him, hey ?   You want to marry him ?

LALAGE (*hardly*).   No.

RAGATZY (*insistently*).   *Yes !*   But you would not curse him with a crippled wife.   (*Moves back and forwards.*)   Some other woman gets him, hey ?   That is not nice for you.   And even if you were married to him he would go to golf and dance with other women, hey ?   That is all the young ones think of nowadays, dance, dance . . . dance !   And they hold each other pretty close too.   It makes them think of marriage, hey ? . . .

LALAGE (*with low intensity*).   You *beast* !

RAGATZY (*standing by bed—sententiously*).   A man is *a* beast.   A dog, a dancing dog.   But what a pity you are a beauty.   It is no good.   It must be jolly torture lying here knowing what a good time you would have—if you were not a cripple.   (*Sits quickly in chair by her.*)   Men would go mad for you.   Throw themselves at your feet.   (*Looking significatively at her deformed foot.*)   You don't want that *now*, hey ?   (*With deliberation.*)   But . . . if I . . . cure you !

LALAGE (*in a sudden outburst, rising to her feet and lurching to the mantel, she stands leaning back against it, her arms outstretched upon it*).   Oh . . . are you a temptation of the devil, or an answer to my prayers ?

RAGATZY (*nodding wisely*).   Half and half.

(*N.B.—From this time* LALAGE *does not use her crutch at all. But moves always supported by leaning on some piece of furniture or some one's arm.*)

LALAGE.   What sort of a man are you ?   Charlatan, liar, trickster—an outsider ?   How am I to believe you ?   How am I to know that you won't tell me you can cure me just to be revenged upon my father ?   And then experiment upon me. . . .   Vivisect me.

RAGATZY (*genuinely*).   No.   I am bad, but not as bad as that. (*Rises to* C.)   See here, I swear to you now, before your God—I will not say that I can cure you unless I am *double sure* I can.   I will not do to you one thing I would not do to my own sister.

(*Re-enter* BASIL, *empty-handed.*)

BASIL (C.).   Lally, Miss Cross is digging out the negatives.   They're great whole-plate things and . . . she's afraid . . .

RAGATZY.   That you smash them.   Eh, stay here, I will go. (*Moves to door.*) . . .   To see the plates is better than the prints.

BASIL.   I'll go with you. (*Moving up to door for* RAGATZY.)

RAGATZY.   Oh no . . . no . . . no.   You stay.

BASIL.   Yes ?

(RAGATZY *crosses above* BASIL *who turns, looking at him, and follows him up to door.* RAGATZY *goes out, indicating to* BASIL *to stay.* BASIL *understands and crosses to* LALAGE.)

(*Standing by chair.*)   Lally . . .

LALAGE.   Basil, don't look at me like that.   As though you saw me with new eyes.   You *mustn't* . . .

BASIL (*intense feeling, moves chair away—kneels*).   I *must*.   And you must, Lally.   Oh, Lally, see yourself as he can make you. . . .   My dear, he's done such wonders.   I believe he can.   Oh, Lally, even to think of seeing you like that makes me feel . . .   Why, every one will fall in love with you !

LALAGE (*setting her teeth and moaning faintly*).   I know. . . . (*Moving away from* BASIL.)

BASIL.   Lally, if he says he can cure you, you'll tell your father he must let him : won't you ? .

LALAGE.   Basil . . . it will be awful . . . *awful* for him.

BASIL. But glorious for *you*. Oh, Lally, don't you want to *live* ?

LALAGE. So much ! So much ! Because my music wants it just as much as I do. It's half-starved. ʌ My life's so empty,ʌ I want it to be full of everything on earth. All the gorgeous, joyous, happy things. ʌ Basil, what's it *like* to be able to put one foot in front of the other quite easily just like I move my hands ? Oh, Basil, if I could dance so beautifully that all the men were wild to be my partners—dance till the music dances into me, the lilt and swing and rhythm and the love song of it. . . . (*Hears door bang.*) Oh, Basil ! . . .

BASIL. Lally, he's coming now ! (*Rises.*)

LALAGE (*whispering*). Basil, hold me. Don't let my heart . . . break.

(BASIL *clasps her hand to his breast. She leans on him.*)

(*Re-enter* RAGATZY *with a serious face.*)

BASIL (*breathless*). Well ? . . . (*At top of couch.*)

LALAGE (*voiceless*). Tell me. (*Doesn't look at* RAGATZY.)

RAGATZY (C.). *I* can cure you.

(*Two seconds' silence.*)

BASIL (*breathless*). You can !

RAGATZY (*confidently*). I know it.

(RAGATZY *plays this bit dead,* C.)

LALAGE. You're sure ? (*Looking at* RAGATZY.)

RAGATZY. If you are brave.

LALAGE (*almost voiceless*). Pain ?

BASIL (*apprehensively*). Will it *hurt* her ? (*At head of bed.*)

RAGATZY. At first. Then . . . *ter*-rible weariness . . . *terrible* strain. . . .

LALAGE. How long ?

RAGATZY. For one year.

LALAGE. Lying down ?

RAGATZY (*moving slightly towards* LALAGE). Strapped on my Rack so that you cannot move—twelve months. Then I shall say —(*mightily*)—" Rise up and walk."

LALAGE (*involuntarily*). Oh !

BASIL (*rapturously*). Lally !

RAGATZY (*slightly* C.). No more limping, no more lurching, no more crutches, no more boots like clumping hoofs. But you shall dance in Cinderella's slippers with your Prince.

BASIL. With me ! With *me* ! Lally, oh Lally ! Float down the room with music playing. Your own music.

LALAGE. Basil, Basil, don't. I can't believe it, oh, I can't, till father says it's true.

RAGATZY (*coolly*). He will say it is not true.

LALLY. What!

RAGATZY (L. *of piano*). He will believe it *is not*. Which will *you* believe?

LALAGE (*drawing a long, deep breath*). You or . . . father!

STURDEE'S VOICE (*off*). Certainly, Miss Cross, 'phone Mr. Helmore that I am back.

(*Enter* STURDEE, *bearing a big bunch of roses and packet of choice-looking chocolates. He looks very cheerful and genial in his stately way, and very happy to be home again.* RAGATZY *walks to piano.*)

LALAGE (*with a little gasping cry that is only half of gladness*). Father!

(BASIL *moves* R. *of couch.*)

STURDEE (*going to her*). Lally, my darling, they wouldn't let me bring you any coals from Newcastle, so I got you these . . . and these . . . from your favourite shop.

(BASIL *drops* R. *of bed. Says* "How do you do, sir.")

Well, Basil, have you two been getting through some work? And has this gentleman been helping you? (*Bows courteously.*)

(RACATZY *bows and begins softly touching notes and running fingers through his hair like a professional musician.* STURDEE *stands on the hearthrug in his favourite attitude, with his eyeglasses in one hand to tap on the other for greater emphasis.*)

My dear, aren't you going to introduce us?

(BASIL *takes flowers from* LALLY *and puts them on mantelpiece.* LALAGE *and* BASIL *look desperately at each other.* RAGATZY'S *mouth twists into a concealed grin. He shuts down lid over keys of piano.*)

LALAGE (*heroically*). Father, this isn't music. It's . . . Mr. . . .

RAGATZY (*rising up level with* STURDEE—*in grating voice*). Anton Rag-at-zy. (*Sits with folded arms on keyboard. Bows.*)

(*Pause.*)

STURDEE (*sharply*). The surgical-instrument maker?

RAGATZY (*coolly*). Also I make miracles.

STURDEE (*majestically*). May I ask what you are doing in my house.

RAGATZY (*with a bow and flourish*). Placing my professional services at the feet of your daughter.

STURDEE (*contemptuously majestic*). Sir, she does not need them.

RAGATZY. Mister sir, I think she does. . . . You are not blind, hey? (*Pointing.*) Look at that . . . can you mend it?

Sturdee (*emphatically stern and bitter*). No one can.

Ragatzy (*coolly*). Then I am no one. (*Moving down* L.C.)

Sturdee. What?

Ragatzy (*coolly positive*). I can cure her.

Sturdee (*trenchantly incredulous*). How?

Ragatzy (*more coolly*). I will not tell you.

Sturdee. You will not tell *me*? (*Following* Ragatzy.)

Ragatzy. No.

Lalage. Mr. Ragatzy . . . please. (*Motions for crutch to* Basil, *who gives it her below couch.*)

Ragatzy (*making the " o " roll out enormously*). N—O. I tell him nothing. But I will show him . . . what I can do alone.

Lalage. Alone? (*Rises.*)

Ragatzy (*nodding*). Yes . . . *Ay*—lone.

Sturdee. Sir, do you mean . . . ?

Ragatzy. I mean that I do not require doctors. Therefore I will have none of *them*.

Lalage. Not even father.

Ragatzy. No.

Lalage (*blankly*). Why not? (*Fear.*)

Ragatzy (*shrewdly*). Because he would want the credit and *I* want it, *ALL*. They shall not make me their mechanic to manufacture glory for them. That is what they want. I know them. Bah!

Sturdee. Sir, will you leave my house? (*Crosses to door and opens it.*)

Ragatzy. Mr. Sir, my twenty minutes. (*Up* c. *addressing* Sturdee.)

Sturdee. Twenty minutes? (*Drops down* L.)

Lalage. Father, I promised.

Basil. She did, sir.

Ragatzy (*nodding*). So she must hear me . . . for still another five. Listen to me. . . . What good are you to me, you, Mr. Sturdee's daughter—(*to* Lally),—unless I have the headlines " Most famous English surgeon cannot cure his daughter. But Ragatzy has done it." (*Facing* Sturdee.)

Sturdee. Advertisement! (*Above piano* L.)

Ragatzy. I must *have* advertisement! Bah! what are they, all these papers? Hens that cackle when some one else has laid an egg! But who shall find the egg without the cackle? (*Says this to* Sturdee.)

Lalage (*indignant*). Do you suppose I'll let you put me on a poster? (Ragatzy *to face* Lally.) Use my name . . . and father's?

Ragatzy (*quietly*). Or not be cured.

Lalage. Oh! (*Sinks down lower—at foot of bed.*)

Sturdee (*quietly*). Like Captain Wycherly.

RAGATZY (*snarling*—L. *of bed* C.). Ach! I knew you would say that. I tell you it is because I fail with that poor boy, who was more, much more worse than is your daughter, I know that I can cure her. I have learnt. Yes, learnt.

STURDEE. Sir, I ask you once more—will—you—leave—my house?

RAGATZY (*crosses to* STURDEE). Yes . . . but not your daughter in it.

STURDEE. Do you imagine you can make her come to *you*?

RAGATZY (*slowly—to* STURDEE). I shall not try. (*To* LALLY.) I shall leave that to Nature and to—(*looking significatively*)—Mr. Basil Owen. (*Turn to* R. *from* C.)

LALAGE. Do you know that you are—diabolically—clever?

RAGATZY (*with satisfaction*). I am not a fool . . . nor a physician.

STURDEE. Sir, you can be what you like outside my house.

RAGATZY (*moving up* C.). Then she shall come outside. . . . (*Round to look at* LALLY.)

STURDEE. What!

RAGATZY (*to* STURDEE). Come to me, I tell you, because your hands are empty. And in mine I hold her health, her youth. (*To* LALLY.) You are *so* lovely, I *want* to make you as God meant you should be . . . you beautiful, you broken thing. But you are *his* daughter. Therefore listen to me, you, Lalage . . . unless you come to me alone and put yourself in these two hands, and no one else's, I will not touch you. Not if you kneel and wash my boots with tears.

(*All stand* R. *of* STURDEE. BASIL *at foot of bed*.)

STURDEE (*striding majestically forward*). Will you go, sir?

RAGATZY (*down two paces, then up to door*). *Yes*, Mister the Lord Marble Arch. (*To* STURDEE *up* C.) You will not meet me as your equal. Very well. I will not meet you till I make you say I am your master . . . till I drag you down like Samson. . . . Now you know, and now I go. (*Turning at door*.) To wait until she comes. (*Exits*.)

(STURDEE *following to door, imperiously. Strides out and disappears*.)

LALAGE (*in a whisper*). Oh, what a man!

BASIL (*soft and urgent*). Lally, *will* you go?

LALAGE (*moaning*). I can't go back on father. Can't desert him.

BASIL. He deserted *you*. Are you going to let him spoil your life again? And *mine*? (*Sits on couch* R. *of* LALAGE.) My dear, I want you. I didn't know I wanted you till now. You want me, don't you, Lally? Enough to bear the pain. I'd bear it for you, if I could. If you tell me you can't face it I won't ask you. But if it's only so as not to hurt your father. . . . (*Kneels* R. *of* LALAGE. Kiss me, kiss me, Lally! And then I'll know you *will*! (*Sitting*) *on edge of bed, she lifts her face as though to meet his waiting lips, then, moving, lets her head fall back before she touches them. He rises to his feet as* STURDEE *re-enters, looking very stern.*)

(BASIL *backs to fireplace.*)

STURDEE (*coming* C.). Lalage, Pritchard tells me you gave *orders* that this man was to be let in. Is that true ? Did you know who he was ?

LALAGE (*with emphasis*). Yes . . . but it was a trick.

BASIL (*eagerly*). She had to because . . .

STURDEE (*holding up his hand*). Thank you. (*Pause.*) Leave us, please. (*He walks to piano* L.)

BASIL (*leaning over her*). Do you want me ? Shall I stay ?

LALAGE. *No.* Not now . . . but . . . wait. . . .

BASIL (*low and urgent*). I will. Oh, Lally, *stick* it ! Think of all it means. (*Kisses her passive hand with fervent lips, then goes out swiftly* L.)

(STURDEE, *who has been standing by the window looking out with steadily unseeing eyes, turns slowly round and paces* C.)

STURDEE (*facing* LALLY). Did you believe this fellow when he told you he could cure you ?

LALAGE (*slowly*). I—liked—to hear it. It was so *new*, that it was—beautiful.

STURDEE (*approaching her—with solemn earnestness*). Lalage . . . *nothing* can be done.

LALAGE (*beginning an hysterical laugh—as before—turns away*). I've heard that so often. But I never get used to it. It always reminds me of the first notes of the Dead March in Saul.

STURDEE (*relentless*). Do you believe me ?

LALAGE (*slowly*). I believe that you believe it.

STURDEE (*sitting* L. *of bed—sadly*). My child, I *know*. (*Takes her hand.*) My little girl, ~~my little baby Lally~~, don't you know that even if this fellow could undo my reputation, ruin me by curing you, I should say " Thank God " !

LALAGE. Yes . . . oh, father darling. . . .

STURDEE. Then do you realize that, thinking as I do, I must maintain my opposition to him ? You could not be under this man's treatment and remain under my roof.

LALAGE (*wincing*). *Father !*

STURDEE (*turning away in his chair from* LALLY). For the sake of my patients who trust in me—my reputation . . . I could not even seem to countenance you. If you choose to put yourself into the hands of an unqualified practitioner, without benefit of surgery. . . .

LALAGE (*with a hard little laugh*). I should be in the same position as an unmarried wife.

STURDEE (*facing* LALLY). You would have to leave this house . . . and me.

(*Pause.*)

LALAGE (*slowly*). I've got mother's money and my own. (*Looking straight in front.*)

STURDEE. Lally, Lally, has this man hypnotized you ?

LALAGE. No. But he'd found out from my music I was not—a saint—and so he stirred up all my senses and played on them because he knew . . .

STURDEE (*his face softening*). What ?

LALAGE. Basil. . . . Oh, father, don't you *know* ? (*Looks at* STURDEE.)

STURDEE (*sitting beside her*). Yes . . . yes . . .

LALAGE (*in a whisper*). Basil . . . I want him.

(*Pause.*)

STURDEE (*sorrowfully*). *Can't* you be content, my child, with your career . . . your music ?

LALAGE. Basil's both ! What's my music worth without his lyrics ? He makes my music speak and I make his songs sing. Neither of us did any good alone. But together . . .

STURDEE. You needn't marry him to work with him.

LALAGE (*not looking at* STURDEE). Not if he didn't marry either. But he will. Then, do you think his wife will ever stand *my* being all I am to him ? Do you think I could bear *her* being all I'm not . . . Am I to let him have *her* body *and* my soul ?

STURDEE (*moved*). No . . . no.

LALAGE (*turns to* STURDEE *for the first time—unsteadily*). If he's happy with her . . . I must let him go. But if he's not . . . and he comes back to me . . . *Father, I'm human.* . . .

STURDEE. Yes, dear, I know.

LALAGE. It would be such a triumph. And I love him. . . . So much . . . that I won't marry him . . . unless . . .

STURDEE (*laying his hand on hers*). My dear child, he isn't worthy of you, if he doesn't know that you've got qualities of mind, and soul. . . .

LALAGE (*bitterly*). Souls don't count with men—in marriage, father, only bodies. If you were a lame woman you'd soon find out that.

STURDEE (*earnestly emphatic*). Don't believe it, Lally. Don't believe it. It's a woman's qualities that win a good man's love.

LALAGE (*terribly*). I don't want a good man's love. I want a young man's passion.

STURDEE (*rises—crosses* c.). Lalage. . . . You don't know what you're saying !

LALAGE (*hardly*). All the things that all my life I haven't said !

STURDEE (*putting her words away with a gesture as though they hurt and shocked him*). Your mother's daughter ! (C.)

LALAGE. Wants what *she* had. What *you* gave her. Wasn't it a young man's passion that flung away from England, leaving everything—country, career, and . . . child ? (*He rises and turns away—crosses up* C. *to window*.) A good man would have bleated "The Lord gave and the Lord taketh away : blessed be the Name of the Lord." And stayed at home and bathed the baby. (*Exclamation from* STURDEE *to bring* LALLY *round*.)

(*Pause. She hides her face. He covers his eyes with his hand*.)

I didn't mean . . . *that*, but . . . (*Almost inaudibly*.) Oh, father ! —if you only had.

STURDEE (*moves round head of couch and sits beside* LALLY, *just behind her, his arm round her. With an effort, yet with a certain relief*). My child . . . I've never known whether you knew.

LALAGE. Oh, yes ! I made old Nanna tell me as soon as ever I began to wonder. And then I thought about it.

STURDEE (*putting his arms round* LALAGE, *who nestles up to him*). Lally, have you ever thought that I've forgiven myself ?

LALAGE. No. The way you loved me told me that. And I knew that you were always asking for my forgiveness, but you couldn't speak. We couldn't either of us, could we ? All these years.

STURDEE (*brokenly*). Lally !

LALAGE. Only I've tried to tell you . . . tried to make you understand. I never blamed you . . . never questioned . . . just accepted because it was you . . . it was . . . right. I've never wanted any father in the world but you. And now . . . I wouldn't have you have loved mother any the less . . . or any other way. For if you had I shouldn't have been born with such a power of passion in me.

(STURDEE *crosses to fireplace*.)

STURDEE. Lally, for a man who doesn't love you !

LALAGE (*coldly unemotional*). Father, before you or any other man can throw that stone at Basil, ask yourselves whether you would want to marry a woman who was a cripple. Would you *ever* have fallen in love with mother if she'd been lame ?

STURDEE (*shuddering—crosses* C. *down stage*). She was the lightest . . . swiftest . . .

LALAGE. And if she hadn't been . . . you wouldn't have . . . because you couldn't . . . Could you ?

STURDEE (*turns to* LALAGE C.). My dear . . . don't ask me.

LALAGE (*coldly and slowly*). I won't, because I know. I've known it ever since I've read a sentence in a book—" Men are more

D

physically particular than women "—and it struck me like a blow that it was true.

(STURDEE *crosses back to chair to try to comfort* LALAGE.)

Father, Basil can't love me while I'm like this, though he wants to. And I can't blame him, because I know that if I were a man I wouldn't want to marry—(*taps breast*)—me. I should want a woman beautifully perfect . . . the sort of woman Basil wants. Oh, father, I could make him marry me for pity if I'd played on his chivalry. I could have made half a dozen men. But I can't stoop to conquer.

STURDEE (*sadly*). Lally, Lally, why are you so proud?

LALAGE. Because my life's been one long unending humiliation that has crucified my soul. And this man comes and tells me, he can take the nails out, lift me from the cross.

STURDEE (*strongly*). He can do nothing for you, Lally. He doesn't understand enough of surgery to know he can't. There's nothing *known* . . .

(STURDEE *begins to turn and she stops him.*)

LALAGE. But there's the Unknown . . . always. (*With an effort.*) Father . . . do you remember after I'd been to Moritz, you told me there was no more hope! I mustn't even pray. That seemed to shut out God. But . . . father . . . Moritz cured children no one else could? This man cures grown-ups Moritz couldn't. . . . God goes *on.*

STURDEE (*slowly and quietly*). And I am left behind. (*Moves up* C.)

(*Enter* PRITCHARD.)

PRITCHARD. Mr. Helmore and Mr. Frederick Ladd to see you, sir.
STURDEE. I'll come—No, show them in here.
PRITCHARD. Sir Nathan Israel is here too in the library wanting to see you on a private matter.
STURDEE. Show him in also. All of them——
PRITCHARD. Very good, sir. (*Exits.*)
STURDEE (*crosses to* LALAGE, *top of couch*). Lally, you've got to hear what they think of this man and his conduct. I can't trust myself.
LALAGE. Mr. Ladd knows all about him, doesn't he?
STURDEE (*standing by fireplace*). Yes, but Helmore's opinion is worth ten of his . . . and Israel's the most advanced and brilliant of all the younger men. Hear what they say.
LALAGE. I'd believe Sir Nathan. . . .

(*Enter* SIR NATHAN ISRAEL, *grave and concerned, followed by* LADD, *self-controlled but nervous, and* HELMORE, *indignant and excited.*)

ISRAEL. My dear Miss Lalage . . . we didn't expect the pleasure . . .

LADD. How do you do, Miss Lally. (*Up* R.C.)

HELMORE (C.). Forgive this intrusion . . . Sturdee, we really came to tell you about what happened yesterday after you'd gone.

STURDEE (*grimly*). Have you heard what's happened here to-day before I came ?

HELMORE. Yes. Young Owen's told us . . . Ragatzy's been here.

STURDEE. And informed my daughter he can cure her. (*Moves round to fire-place.*)

LADD. He has !

HELMORE (*snorting by chair* L. *of bed*). Infernal impudence.

LALAGE. Mr. Helmore, if you were like me . . . if you'd suffered all I've suffered . . . and knew as I know what I've got before me . . . you wouldn't characterize any offer to cure you as . . . exactly—impudent.

HELMORE. No . . . No ! I mean, of course, his coming here.

STURDEE. He has the colossal hardihood to insist upon my daughter placing herself entirely in his hands.

HELMORE. Good God !

LADD (*bitterly*). He's told all my patients they can choose between us.

LALAGE. Which have they chosen ?

LADD (*more bitterly*). Him, of course. They know that I can't cure them.

LALAGE. He's a pretty magnificent mechanic.

LADD (*up* C. *to window*). He's a scoundrel.

LALAGE. Mr. Ladd, do you think that I, or any other cripple, would care about the moral character of any man who has the power to cure us ? *Has* he that power ?

STURDEE. Has he the *knowledge* ?

ISRAEL. Of mechanics to an nth degree. (*Moving down* L.C.)

HELMORE. But he's an outsider !

(LADD *moves up* C.)

LALAGE. Well . . . what am I ? Aren't I an outsider too ? Outside the common human joys of life and love.

HELMORE (*with gentleness and understanding*). I know it's very hard for you, but . . .

LALAGE. Mr. Helmore, Sir Nathan. There is such a thing as the indecent exposure of the soul. But, as you're doctors, I suppose it's quite all right for you to see mine . . . naked. (*Drawing a deep breath, then starkly.*) I want to . . . marry.

(*Pause.*)

HELMORE (*glancing at* STURDEE *carefully*). There's no reason why you shouldn't.

LALAGE. Not from the man's point of view ?

(ISRAEL *turns head away—pause.*)

(*With a curious dragging change of tone that makes him start.*) Vincent
. . . do you remember a long time ago, when we used to see a good
deal of each other and you told me I had the most beautiful and
wonderful soul of any woman you had ever met ?

HELMORE (*unhappily*). Did I ?

LALAGE. But you married a woman who you thanked God to
me could go mountain-climbing with you.

HELMORE (*turns over* L. *shoulder towards door—constrained*). I'd
better go. I can do no good here. (*Checked by* NATHAN.)

(STURDEE *places his hand on* LALLY'S *shoulder.*)

LALAGE. None of you can. You're *men* . . . you doctors—so
you know men *are* like that.

(HELMORE *drops down by piano,* R. *of it.*)

STURDEE (*below couch*). Israel . . . (*Crosses to* LALLY *and
stands* L. *of couch.*)

ISRAEL (*gently insistent*). My dear Miss Lalage . . . won't you
listen to me for one moment ?

LALAGE (*breathing defiance*). Are you going to tell me lies ?

ISRAEL (*earnestly*). No, no. The truth.

LALAGE. Go on.

ISRAEL (*slowly*). I have known for some time that this thing
must come to you.

LALAGE. This man ?

ISRAEL. This crisis. I have watched you grow into a strong
and splendid woman—seen your temperament, your warmth, your
heart. . . . All meant for love—to be poured out in love. But
baffled, and I know that for such women—if they do not marry,
there are temptations—both of life—and death.

LALAGE. You mean you were afraid that I might shoot myself—
or take a lover. Oh, I've thought of both. But either would be
too much of a compliment to your damn sex.

(HELMORE *moves below piano.*)

STURDEE. My child ! My child !

LALAGE (*rises*). I'm not a child—and I can't be a woman—I'm
held back. (*To* ISRAEL.) Sir Nathan, you understand, because
your race . . .

ISRAEL (*nods head gently*). We, too, have been in bondage.

LALAGE. "And by the waters of Babylon they asked *you* for
your songs."

ISRAEL. Because of that, I came to-day to ask your father, if
we could not use this man's invention, in any way to set you free.

STURDEE (*positively*). No.

ISRAEL. Sturdee. Do you realize that he *has* done by mechanism
what we have failed to do by surgery !

[Handwritten margin note: Israel goes across to Lalage]

LALAGE. Father, it's what I told you. God goes *on*!
HELMORE (*ironically*). Hand-in-hand with Ragatzy.

(NATHAN *turns up slightly to head of couch.*)

LALAGE. That's what I don't know. But I must know it. Mr.
Ladd, you know this man, you've worked with him.

.(LADD *is above piano* L.)

(*The door is quietly opened by* RAGATZY, *who stands listening intently,
unperceived.*)

LALAGE. Can he cure me or do you think he'd tell me lies . . .
just for the sake of getting me to go to him?
HELMORE. Yes. (*Hotly.*)
RAGATZY No.

(*All turn to look,* NATHAN *drops down level with* LADD.)

(*furiously*). I have told her that I will not lie to her.

(*He comes down* C., *followed by* BASIL, *looking very anxious.*)

STURDEE. Sir, you dare to come back? (*At foot of bed.*)
BASIL (L. *of* RAGATZY). Sir, I let him in.
STURDEE (*behind his teeth—turning away*). You!! . . .
RAGATZY. I see him standing at the window, when I came back
to put a letter to your daughter in your box. I make sign to him to
come to speak to me. But when he tells me all the misters surgeons
are here to tell her lies about me—I say I will come in to answer
them. (*To* LALAGE.) What have they told you?

(LADD *slowly drops down* L. *of piano.*)

LALAGE. What have you written to me?

(*Pause.*)

RAGATZY (*slowly*). That I will not make advertisement of . . .
you.
LALAGE. Not if you cure me? Why not?

(*Pause.*)

RAGATZY. Because you are so—so—I would not make you. . . .
It is enough you make them recognize me.
HELMORE. So . . . (*truculently*)—you're climbing down . . . are
you? (*Turning in front of piano.*)
RAGATZY (*to* HELMORE). *What* do you say? You *mean* . . .
HELMORE. You're going to keep this very quiet, aren't you?
So that there'll be nothing said if you don't cure her.
LALAGE (*magnificently*). There *shall* be. You've challenged

father, now I challenge you. Will you have it put in the papers
now that you can cure me ?

RAGATZY. Beforehand ?

LALAGE. *Yes.* So, if you fail—they'll placard it in headlines
just as big as if . . . you're right. . . . Who's going to find the
egg without the cackle. . . . Do you suppose if you succeed I
don't want all the world to *know* ? . . . To tell the hopeless cases
everywhere that they can hope ! And if you fail . . . that I won't
have your failure blazoned forth and justify my father.

RAGATZY (*down* C.). I shall not fail. Bah, I am not afraid.
Yes, I *will* put it in, to-morrow . . . next day . . . I tell you all
that you can come, this time next year . . . and see her taken off
the Rack and *walk* ! I know myself, what I can do.

STURDEE (*terribly*). You—can—do—*nothing* !

(*As* RAGATZY *moves up* C. *he signals* BASIL *to go to* LALAGE.)

LALAGE (*despairingly*). Oh, father !

BASIL (*crosses* R. *to* LALAGE). Lally, he *has* cured people that
they said he couldn't.

(ISRAEL *moves to head of bed.*)

RAGATZY (*nodding*). And that is not a lie. Ask Mr. Ladd (C.).

LALAGE. Mr. Ladd, this man, says he can cure me. Father
says he can't. Which do you believe ?

LADD (*hesitating*). I—Miss Sturdee—in *your* case your father's
opinion *must* be . . .

STURDEE (*terribly*). Don't equivocate, sir—answer.

LADD (C., *doggedly*). I believe in—Ragatzy. (*Moving away* L.).

(*Warning for Curtain.*)

LALAGE. And I believe in God. (*To* STURDEE.) The God who
does things. And gives people who believe the power to do them.
I'm going to *believe*—I'm going . . .

STURDEE (*with sudden pleading*). Lally ! Lally ! My child !

LALAGE. Father darling. (*With emotion.*) You're absolutely
right. I couldn't stay here. . . .

STURDEE. Lally, are you going to leave me ?

LALAGE. Do you forbid ?

STURDEE. Forbid !

HELMORE (*urgently*). Miss Lalage, it's madness.

ISRAEL (*above* STURDEE, *by couch*). *If* he makes you worse !

LALAGE. Then I shall know I never *can* be better. . . . Never
marry. . . . (*To* STURDEE.)

RAGATZY. You *can* be better. Can be well. Listen, I have a
house where I have had another patient—rooms . . . vacant now . . .

(BASIL *draws* LALAGE *away from her father.* LALAGE's *head gradually
raising up.*)

. . . with balcony that overlooks the Regent's Park—where you shall be all day—all night long—in the open air.

BASIL.   And I'll come to see you—Lally—always—every day.

(LALAGE *glances at her father and hesitates.*)

LALAGE (*moving away from her father*).   Oh, Basil!   (*Lifts her lips to his.*)

BASIL (*joyful*).   That means you will!

RAGATZY.   Come!

(LALAGE, *supported on her left by* BASIL, *begins to move up to door.*)

STURDEE (*taking a step after them*).   Lally!

LALAGE (*turning as she stands* C.).   Father . . . oh father darling . . . understand . . . I must.   (*Making a tremendous gesture with outstretched right hand towards him.*)   I want LIFE!

(LALAGE *and* BASIL *go out together.*   RAGATZY *in triumph is about to follow quickly.*   STURDEE *follows up to* RAGATZY.)

STURDEE (*striding forward indignantly*).   Sir, you are taking my daughter . . .

RAGATZY (*turning magnificently in doorway*).   I am taking my degree!   A bigger one than you have. . . .   A.D.F. . . .   Hey? . . .   "After . . . Doctor's Fail"!!! . . .

(*He goes out, pulling door shut behind him.*)

CURTAIN.

To face page 57]

ACT III

Scene I

Scene.—Lalage's *Flat, Regent's Park, N.W.*

Time.—*Three months later. Evening.*

(*Down* R. *there is a 6-foot wall, with a door* (R.L.E.) *leading to* Madame Klost's *and the servants' apartments. At right angles to this, and running across stage at a slight rake, is a 15-foot piece with four-fold folding glass doors, beyond which is the balcony. These doors fold on to the stage, and not on to the balcony. The doorpiece is joined by an 8-foot plain wall, which runs almost directly up and down stage. The angle of the glass doors and the plain wall is approximately 9-feet from carpet cut. An 8-foot double doorpiece joins this at back* L.C. *The left wall of the room joins this up stage with a door* (L.U.E.) *and a fireplace in the* C. *of the wall. Down* R. *in the angle formed by the door* (R.L.E.) *and the glass doors is a small table, with a silver clock, matches, cigarettes, book, handkerchief, etc., and a small chair.*

Approximately 6 feet from the glass doors, and up stage is parapet of the balcony, showing the backcloth of tree-tops in Regent's Park beyond. The balcony is covered in at top and on R. *by a striped awning. On the balcony is the Rack on which* Lalage *is lying, the foot of which is against the doorpost almost* C. *There is room for* Ragatzy *to pass around the head of the Rack to behind it, where there is a standard lamp.*

Flush against the 8-foot plain wall is a long Italian buffet table, empty in the first scene, and covered with flowers in Scene II. Between the door L.U.E. *and the fireplace is a small table and chair, with papers, etc., and below fireplace* L. *a small writing-desk on which stands a table-lamp, cigarette-box, matches, letters, etc., for* Ragatzy, *and a small hall chair. There are brackets on the 8-foot plain wall and above fireplace. Switches for same down* R. *and on* L. *wall.*

Lalage *lies strapped to the Rack, her head lying on a little flat pillow, covered with snowy draperies. She wears a dressing-jacket of pale blue silk and swansdown, falling back from her night-gown, and a little close-fitting cap of lace. She looks very white and weary, but she is not asleep, for she sighs and keeps on moving restlessly as though she were straining against the strappings. In the distance*

57

across the park, the band is playing the music of a languorous waltz. As the curtain rises MADAME KLOST, *dressed as a nurse attendant, is quietly sitting by head of Rack.*)

(*Enter* RAGATZY C., *who beckons to* MADAME KLOST. *She tiptoes across stage to him.*)

RAGATZY (*in an undertone*). Why did you telephone for me to come ? Has she some pain ?

MADAME KLOST (*ditto—shaking head*). She says no . . . but she is restless.

RAGATZY. Ach ! She must not be ! She *must* lie absolutely still. She knows that very well. Why does she not ?

MADAME KLOST. I think to-night that she is sad a little.

RAGATZY. Sad ? Why is she sad ? I will not *have* her sad. Why is not Basil Owen here to make her happy. My great goodness, does he not know that is what he is *for* ?

MADAME KLOST. To-night, it is the Danse des Fleurs at Claridge's. He goes to it. But first, he say, perhaps he will come here to say good night to her.

(*Band ceases.*)

RAGATZY (*with angry scorn*). Perhaps . . . perhaps . . . *perhaps*. He must not say perhaps to her. He must not leave her in uncertainty. Does he not know that is the worse thing that can be for her. The devil destroy him ! Is he all a fool !

LALAGE (*in a tired but clear voice, as she turns her head and calls from without*). Is that *you*, Mr. Ragatzy ? At this hour ? Nearly nine o'clock ?

RAGATZY (*aside, grimly*). Yes. She is watching every minute until she knows it is too late for him to come. (*Aloud, cheerily.*) Aha ! You recognize my voice ? (*Goes to window.*)

LALAGE (*faintly smiling*). I recognize your language. Who's a fool ?

RAGATZY (*by left end of glass doors* C., *imperturbably*). A friend of Madame Klost's . . . a man called Richardson who lives at Putney.

(*Music stops.*)

LALAGE (*wearily*). Oh, no one I know. Why have you come ?

RAGATZY (*standing by door at foot of Rack*). Because I pass here on my way from dining with the Prince of Wales. No . . . no, it is agreed, hey, that I do not tell you any fibs, very well, the truth. (*Stands by her looking keenly at her.*) I come, since Madame Klost . . . she makes you a good little night nurse, hey ? And now all the pain is finished, every time you see her, you can say : " I only must lie here . . . quite still as I have promised Mr. Ragatzy, and one day I shall rise up and walk as she did and as well as she does."

LALAGE. I can't believe it . . . sometimes.

RAGATZY (*strongly*). You must believe it always. You *are* safe.
Look at me and say . . . " I know I am . . . in *your* hands, Anton
Ragatzy."

(*Holds both hands out to her. She touches them gently.*)

LALAGE (*slowly*). They are very wonderful, your hands. . . .

RAGATZY (*roundly*). You must believe it *always*, you are safe !
(*Lifting pearl chain from her breast.*) Hullo ! What is this ? Something new. Good imitations, hey ? (*Feels them.*) No, they are
real ! My heavens ! If your Basil Owen's poetry buys you these
I will make rhymes, not Racks.

LALAGE. They're not from Basil. (*In a low intense tone.*) They
came yesterday. Because it was my birthday.

RAGATZY (*roughly*). Who from ?

LALAGE (*briefly*). Father.

RAGATZY (*ruefully*). Ah—ow. (*Slowly.*) That makes you think
of him, hey ? You have not heard at all till this ?

LALAGE (*briefly*). No.

RAGATZY. Did you have a letter ?

LALAGE. Oh no. He wouldn't write. I know that. Only a
slip of paper with just " God bless my little girl." (*She looks into
space and speaks unsteadily.*) I write to him long letters every week,
of course, but . . . I'm missing a whole year of his dear life and . . .
he isn't young. . . . (*A sob shakes her whole frame.*)

RAGATZY. Don't cry . . . don't cry . . . you must *not* cry.
He is as strong as horses. You must not think of this one year.
But of all the other years when he shall be so happy because his
girl is well. . . . (*Plunges down* L. *into room again, shaking his
head and clenching fists. In an undertone to* MADAME KLOST.) That
fellow leaves her to lie here lonely, all alone . . . to think of how
she wants her father. My hell ! but he shall pay to me for
this !

(MADAME KLOST *remains listening intently down* L. *as he turns again
to the balcony, speaking with cheerful reassuring confidence.*)

Well . . . well . . . what was I saying ? . . . That I have come
here because the little Klost has told me on the 'phone that you are
so restless that she does not think that you will settle down unless I
talk to you. So when I meet your Mr. Basil Owen downstairs I
tell him he must not come up to more excite you.

MADAME KLOST (*bewildered beneath her breath, frightened*). But
. . . that is not true . . .

(*He makes an angry imperious movement behind his back with his* L.
hand to silence her.)

LALAGE (*with an eager gasp*). Then he *did* come.

RAGATZY (*lying smoothly*). Of course he did. He told you that he would.

LALAGE (*sighing contentedly*). Oh no. He only said he *might*.

(RAGATZY *watches her keenly and sees how she now lies still as though her mind and body were at rest. He nods at* MADAME KLOST *with greatest satisfaction, regardless of her frightened face.*)

RAGATZY. And so you wondered if he would. And when a woman wonders if a man will come she wonders if he loves her. But now he has come now you know, hey?

LALAGE (*softly*). Yes. He came.

RAGATZY (*seriously*). Oh, he was terribly upsetted when I say he cannot come up. He say he do not want to go to this damn dance, and all the women in the world but you are sawdust dolls.

LALAGE (*with shining eyes*). Did he really say that?

RAGATZY. Ask him to-morrow, he will tell you " yes." He sends you *all* his love and twenty thousand kisses.

LALAGE (*lovingly*). *All* his love.

RAGATZY (*firmly*). All. And says, good night, sleep well and dream of him. (*Gently.*) Now you can rest, hey? Go to sleep because you know he loves you.

LALAGE (*blissfully*). Yes.

RAGATZY (*turning into room cheerfully*). Madame Klost, you can now go to supper. She is going to sleep. (*He drives her to the door* R.L.E.)

MADAME KLOST (*frightened*). But it is all lies you tell her.

RAGATZY (*grimly*). It is going to be the truth. I promise and vow some things in Mr. Basil Owen's name he shall make good. Go, put out the light.

(*Exit* MADAME KLOST C., *switching off light at door. The room is now in half darkness as the evening glow seen through the windows has faded into soft blue darkness. The standard lamp is alight on the balcony and in the room a small shaded lamp is alight on table down* L. RAGATZY *gets cigarette from table and lights it, holding the match between his hands so that light illumines his face as with varying expressions he listens to* LALAGE'S *speech, facing down stage.*)

LALAGE (*earnestly*). Mr. Ragatzy, you mustn't think he's neglecting me. He's been so good . . . so good. I couldn't do without him while there was the pain. But now there isn't going to be pain any more I thought I ought to let him go. He's such a happy darling. It's been so dreadful for him.

RAGATZY (*letting out match*). To see your soul shine out. (*Going up* C.) To watch your spirit conquer. And for him?

LALAGE. To see my body suffer. He hates suffering. It's so ugly. A woman's body should be beautiful and happy.

RAGATZY. You think a woman's body is the only thing that

matters to a man. (*Leaning against door of french window* C., *blowing cigarette rings.*)

LALAGE. It's only when her body matters that her soul does.

RAGATZY (*grimly*). Yes. I think the inside must be as pretty as the outside when I married.

LALAGE (*delicately*). Oh yes, I remember. . . . You said you *had* been married.

RAGATZY. Oh, she was a darling little kitten—was my wife. A lollipop. A little body made of all white softness to be cuddled. Baby big blue eyes and yellow curls, a little wet red mouth just like a kiss.

LALAGE (*gently*). You must have loved her.

RAGATZY (*nodding*). We were boy and girl together. Very poor. And . . . phoo . . . for three months it was heaven. Then—(*his voice rasps and hardens*)—she sell herself—*and* me—*and* my honour to my best friend . . . for three dollars.

LALAGE (*shocked*). Oh ! . . . You . . . of course . . . you left her.

RAGATZY (*contemptuously*). Leave her. No. I kicked them out together. Pah !

LALAGE (*gently*). I'm sorry.

RAGATZY. And you will be sorry also for your Basil Owen. Because he will be married to an angel. What would be your price to be unfaithful to him ? I wonder ?

LALAGE (*simply*). I don't know.

RAGATZY (*goes round head of Rack out on to balcony and stands above her*). I wish I could find out.

LALAGE. What for ?

RAGATZY (*grinning and shrugging*). For myself, of course. (LALAGE *laughs.*) Do you not know if you would give me one of the so lovely looks you give to him that I would jump for joy over the balcony. (*He is more than half in earnest as he says this, looking down keenly at her.*)

LALAGE (*smiling*). Please *don't*. I want you.

RAGATZY (*grimly*). To make your body well and beautiful for him.

LALAGE. Yes. Because . . . I think . . . he wants me.

RAGATZY (*roundly*). You think ! I *know*. He wants you so much that he will dance no more—till you can dance with him. He says he will come round to-morrow very early to tell you that it is no good to be with other girls while all the time he only thinks how you are lying here alone and wants to be with you.

LALAGE (*piteously*). He doesn't want me half as much as I want him. Mr. Ragatzy, I'm selfish . . . but I'm so weak, so tired . . . I can't hold on. . . .

RAGATZY (*quickly and strongly*). He will hold on for you. (*Takes both her passive hands in his.*) And I will hold you for to-night. . . .

I will not leave you till you go to sleep. (*Slowly and magnetically.*) Go to sleep. (*Slips his hand up till he clasps her wrists and strokes her forearms gently and rhythmically with his forefingers.*) See I stroke your pulses till they go to sleep and let you rest. Go to sleep and dream that you are dancing with your boy. Dream until your dreams come true.

LALAGE (*sighing*). It's so long—so long.

RAGATZY (*as before*). It will not be so long if you are sleeping. Sleeping like the Sleeping Princess Beauty. She did not find the hundred years too long to wait, hey? for her prince. . . . Go to sleep. (*Lifts her hands gently to her breast.*) Hold on your father's pearls. They are to comfort you.

LALAGE (*drowsily*). They feel warm and living.

RAGATZY. They press kisses on your fingers from him. (*Making passes over her eyes and stroking her forehead exquisitely delicately with his finger-tips.*) Go to sleep. All through the summer nights. And all the days your boy shall come to you. Because he loves you. Go to sleep . . . until the days of fog and yellow leaves. Then for a little while when all the trees are black and white with frost and he will sit beside you, because he loves you. Go to sleep, for when the crocuses push out of the earth like little golden flames you too shall rise up. Oh, how your boy will love you then—if you will go to sleep now . . . to sleep . . . to sleep . . . to sleep because he loves you, loves you . . . loves you.

(*She sleeps as* RAGATZY *makes one last pass over her eyes. He moves softly to standard lamp, turns it out—spot limes out—then steps quietly into room and as silently as possible, begins to shut french windows.*)

(BASIL *enters—when first door is closed—in full evening dress, holding his opera hat in hand and a light overcoat upon his arm.*)

(*Brackets and batten up.*)

RAGATZY. My God! *Hush!*

BASIL (*in a whisper*). Has she gone to sleep?

RAGATZY (*ditto*). Silence! Don't stir. Don't make a movement. Wait. (*Very gently he draws to the french windows and drops the latch to fasten them.*)

BASIL. Has she gone to sleep? (*He switches on the centre light, goes down* L. *and puts hat and coat on chair.*)

RAGATZY. Yes. Speak quietly.

BASIL (*under breath*). Why? What's the matter? Isn't she so well?

RAGATZY (*roughly*). The matter is . . . (*watches him very keenly*) . . . I shall throw up the case.

BASIL (*aghast*). W—what? . . .

RAGATZY (*fiercely*). Yes. Throw it up . . . because I will not fail.

(*Both over* L. *by fireplace.*)

BASIL. B—but I thought you could not fail now. You'd succeeded—done everything you wanted to . . . you said so.

RAGATZY. I have done, but Nature has not. She must lie here in perfect stillness eight months more . . . till all that I have broken sets—binds together—and all new tissues form as though she were a child again within her mother's womb.

BASIL. But she *is* lying out there.

RAGATZY. She was lying restless—lying stretching—lying straining—lying crying. Crying for her father because you are not there to make her all forget her father and her father's house.

BASIL (*protesting—bewildered*). But I didn't know she wanted me. She said she *wanted* me to go. . . . And I was getting stale . . . so . . .

RAGATZY. And so you leave her to lie here and think, how all she does for you is less to you than some little chorus girl.

BASIL (*strongly*). But Lally knows.

RAGATZY. She is so weak she cannot know—she only feels. Feels that you have another woman whirling in your arms. I tell you I have exhausted all her strength . . . yes, worn it to so fine a thread that if one tear falls on it, it is broken. I would as soon that she should bleed as cry.

BASIL. I didn't know . . . I mean I didn't think. I say, has it really done her any harm?

RAGATZY (*contemptuously*). I have not let it. I have told her lovely lies. I who swore that I would not lie to her! And got her off to sleep by making love to her . . . for you. (*Moves to* L.)

BASIL (*fervently*). She is asleep. Good! . . . (*Crosses* R.C.)

RAGATZY (*with withering scorn*). Good! *Good.* That another man should play the lover to her. What have you in your veins? Red ink and lukewarm water. Good! Come here! Come here. . . . You shall make it good. (*Motions* BASIL *to come nearer to him.* BASIL *slowly does so.*) Give her the love she wants, to give her still the will to win. Bah! That is all that she has to fight with, love . . . your love. My heavens and hell! To think that I am altogether in your hands—you puppy dog.

BASIL (*sneering*). Why don't *you* make love to her?

RAGATZY. It would revolt her, because I am her doctor! She is not flesh and blood to me but clay beneath the potter's fingers. Why do you talk these nonsenses. It is your love she must have to make her heart-beats strong. Or else . . . (*Drops his voice.*) You don't like sick-rooms.

BASIL (*with sincerity*). I don't . . . I hate 'em. But I've stuck it . . . by God I have *stuck* it.

RAGATZY. But if I leave her on your hands a cripple you will have to stick it all your life . . . yes.

BASIL (*dismayed*). What do you mean?

RAGATZY. You cannot give her up because you are a public schoolboy. If you were a cad like me . . . you could desert her.

BASIL. (*breathing hard*). You're damned offensive. (*Crosses L. and picks up coat off chair down L.*) I don't know what you blackguard me like this for. If Lally can't get better without me being with her always . . . why, of course, I'll stay with her. Of course, I will—I—I love her.

RAGATZY. You swear?

BASIL (*emphatically earnest*). I *swear*.

RAGATZY. Then it will be all right. All right. I know it. And I will tell you something that shall put a little backbone in your spine. *Her father knows it too.*

BASIL (*incredulous*). How do you know?

RAGATZY. If he did not he would not let her stay here. Bah— he would come and carry her away. Yes—in his arms. You think that he would have her sacrificed upon my altar unless he knew that she would rise again? I tell you—No.

BASIL (*delighted*). I say—of course, he wouldn't . . . I never thought of that. But, oh! of course not. He is so fond of her. I say that's splendid—isn't it? Simply splendid.

RAGATZY. You know what you have got to do?

BASIL (*anxiously*). Yes . . . No . . . Tell me.

RAGATZY. You will come to-morrow—early—ten o'clock.

BASIL. Ten. . . . Oh! (*His face falls.*)

RAGATZY. You must seem eager.

BASIL (*heroically*). All right. I will. . . . Ten.

RAGATZY. To tell her that you love her so—you cannot leave her any more. You do not want to dance with any woman till you dance with her.

BASIL (*drawing a deep breath*). Yes.

RAGATZY. But you will say it with conviction, strongly . . . for if you do not—if you fail me—if you make me fail—I will smash every bone within your body into splinters. So you shall be a cripple that no one . . . can cure, not even Ragatzy. Now you can go . . . and dance. . . .

(*Exit* BASIL. *Count four. Door slams without.*)

(RAGATZY, *by french window, notices that* MADAME KLOST *has forgotten the table bearing small clock, book and handbell. He shakes his fist at door through which she went. Then switches off lights by switch below door down* R. *Opens folding doors, fetches small table, and places it beside the head of the Rack by* LALAGE'S R. *hand.*)

(*'Cello solo begins.*)

R sg. puts out lights.
opens balcony curtains
bungs table.

(*Then he goes out to balcony to look at weather. Standing above foot of rack, holds hand out to see if it is raining.* LALAGE *stirs and murmurs:* "BASIL! Basil! Basil!" RAGATZY *comes above rack, and looks down at her. She tosses wearily and still calls with utmost yearning:* "Basil!" *in her sleep.*)

RAGATZY (*imitating* BASIL'S *voice*). Lally darling——
LALAGE. Good night. (*She speaks blissfully and dreamily, contented, lying still again.*)
RAGATZY (*still imitating*). Good night.
LALAGE. Kiss me. . . .

(*She lifts her mouth to seek his* [*Basil's*]. RAGATZY *recoils, then gently bends over her and kisses her. She responds in ecstasy and sinks back on her pillows.* RAGATZY *leaves the balcony and moves down* L. *to fetch his hat. As he puts out hand for hat,* LALAGE *murmurs:* "Basil, Basil." RAGATZY *pauses, his face works. He steels himself to stern resolve, then softly moves up* L. *to double doors. Exit.*)

CURTAIN.

(*Cue for curtain when* RAGATZY *up at door.*)

SCENE II

The same as before, but there is a low couch down L. *quite close to the desk, and a large wicker armchair down* R. *The morning light pours brightly through the open windows, and there are many artistically arranged baskets and bouquets of flowers.*

(RAGATZY *is standing* C., *lighting a cigarette.* BASIL *stands down* R., *also looking very happy.*)

HELMORE (*appearing in doorway up* L.). In here?
RAGATZY. Come in, come in! Good morning!
HELMORE. Good morning. Hallo, Basil. (*Looking round the room as he walks round couch to mantelpiece.*) By Jove! these flowers seem pretty festive. Like a birthday, what?
BASIL. Miss Sturdee says it is the birthday of her life.
RAGATZY. Her new life. (*To* LADD, *who appears in doorway.*) In here, Mr. Ladd.
LADD (*shaking hands*). Well, well, I suppose you've really pulled it off. (*Goes down* L. *and sits on sofa.*)
BASIL. Not a doubt about that, I should say.
RAGATZY. What a triumph for me! The newspapers have let you have that in the collar, eh? . . .

E

HELMORE. And the darling public's simply eating it.

LADD. Ye'd think they fairly hated us, wouldn't you ? And after all, we do work pretty hard, curing them of all the ills they have and haven't got.

HELMORE. We're no good to the sort of damn press they love. If we kill anybody it isn't murder, and if we cure them it's not a miracle.

RAGATZY. I am the miracle. My good heavens, I could not have a better press if I murdered my wife. Did you see all the newspaper reporters waiting downstairs ? . . .

BASIL. And the cinematograph camera-men outside. Going to take Lally walking out of the door and show her on the British Movietone. . . .

HELMORE. Yes : " Doctor's daughter cured by charlatan."

LADD. " Miss Lalage Sturdee trips back to her Harley Street home."

RAGATZY. Then they show you . . . " Exit of subdued surgeons." Never mind, I let you out by the back door, eh ?

HELMORE. Oh, my lord !

BASIL. That's all right, Helmore, you'll be shot again at the wedding.

LADD. And is Mr. Ragatzy to be best man ?

RAGATZY (*pointedly to* BASIL). I always am best man.

BASIL (*as he moves down to chair*). *She* doesn't think so.

RAGATZY. No ? But to-day so many changes are waiting for her. Think, here is a beautiful girl . . . all her life a cripple . . . pitied and shunned by men . . . then suddenly . . . a new world opens and she enters . . . her body as beautiful as her face. What is that going to be like to her ? What a sensation. I see her now going down the street, men turning round. Look at her, what a picture. All that and more to come in one big rush. No human being could resist it, it will go to her head. She will be drunk with it. Oh yes, she may be yours to-day . . . but very soon you will have to win her all over again.

BASIL (*under breath*). Why, damn you . . .

HELMORE (*interfering quickly and tactfully*). Has she walked yet ?

RAGATZY. No. Not one step, that was the bargain, hey ? The surgeons to be present when she is taken off the rack.

(*Voices off outside doors.*)

Ah, someone else come. Who is it ?

LADD. Who else are you expecting ?

RAGATZY. Not the Sir Tollemache. He is an obstinate old ostrich who sticks his head into the sand rather than see the sun rise.

(*Enter* SIR MONTAGUE TOLLEMACHE, *looking distinctly forbidding, but, at the same time, rather pleased with himself.*)

TOLLEMACHE. You did not expect me ?

RAGATZY. No.

TOLLEMACHE (*as he moves down* R. *and sits in the armchair*). I thought not, from the tone of your letter, so I came. I don't like people to think they know exactly what I will or will not do. It makes them think they know too much.

(*Enter* SIR NATHAN ISRAEL.)

RAGATZY. *You* have come ?

ISRAEL (*gravely*). To see.

RAGATZY. Well, you have seen the X-ray photographs. What do you think, eh ?

ISRAEL. It looks like being a very great achievement.

TOLLEMACHE. Humph. Photos don't show everything.

ISRAEL. They would not show it if you had destroyed the nerve power. (*Turns to his colleagues.*)

HELMORE. That's true.

LADD. But they would show . . .

RAGATZY. Bah ! *I* will show you. You shall see her walking just like you do . . . right foot, left foot, right foot, left foot. She shall walk before you and before her father.

TOLLEMACHE (*over shoulder to* BASIL, *who is standing behind him*). Where is she ?

BASIL. In there. (*Opens door* R.U.E.)

RAGATZY. Madame Klost, where are you ? Is Miss Sturdee ready ?

LALAGE (*calling without*). Waiting !

RAGATZY. Come in. The Mister Surgeons all are waiting for you. Bring him down here.

(*Enter* LALAGE, *wheeled down* C. *by* MADAME KLOST *and* BASIL. *She is sitting up, fully dressed, on the rack.*)

LALAGE (*excited and delighted*). You have come, all of you. How nice, how nice. Oh, it's good to see you all again. Mr. Ladd, how are you ? Vincent, you're a forgiving angel, I was a little beast.

HELMORE (*kissing her hand*). I ought to have been shot.

LALAGE. Sir Nathan, I'm so glad.

ISRAEL. Dear Miss Lally, so am I, so are we all, believe me.

(LADD *and* HELMORE, *after greeting* LALAGE, *move on to balcony.* RAGATZY *sits on foot of couch.* ISRAEL *remains above the rack.* TOLLEMACHE, *with a grunt, rises and comes up to* LALAGE.)

LALAGE. Sir Montague, this is an honour.

TOLLEMACHE (*grunting*). Well, my dear, you'll be glad to be taken off this damn gridiron, anyway. Now, Mr. Ragatzy.

LALAGE. No, no, wait a minute. First of all tell me, how is father ?

ISRAEL. Very well.

LALAGE. Not sad, not tired, not older ?

ISRAEL. I think these last two months that he is younger than us all.

LALAGE. *That's* because he knows I'm going to be well ?

RAGATZY. Yes, he knows.

TOLLEMACHE (*to* BASIL, *who has dropped down on his right*). Is he coming here to-day ?

LALAGE. No, I wouldn't ask him. It's for me to go to him.

TOLLEMACHE. Then we can get on.

LALAGE. Oh, please. Think. I've been tied down a whole year and I can't wait another minute.

RAGATZY. You shall not. (*Rises and crosses to couch.*) We begin . . . Sir Tolle, Sir Nathan, excuse me . . . Mr. Ladd, will you undo that bolt ? No, better still, I lift her on to the couch. Madame Klost, take away the rack. (*He lifts her from the rack while* MADAME KLOST, *assisted by* BASIL, *wheels the rack off down* R.) So for the last time, I hold you.

LALAGE (*happily nodding*). Yes.

RAGATZY (*half grim, half laughing*). No. (*He puts her down on the couch while* BASIL, *who has returned, speaks to* HELMORE *and then moves to the head of the couch.*) There now, you can sit up. Sit up, I tell you. By yourself. No, no, do not touch her. (*To* BASIL.) She is quite all right. We have kept her muscles strong and supple with vibration and electric massage. That is right. Arch back your shoulders, stretch out your arms.

LALAGE. Ouf, how gorgeous. I want to put my arms round everybody.

TOLLEMACHE (*as he rises and crosses to her*). And so you shall, my dear.

(*Pushes* BASIL *aside and she laughingly puts her arms round his neck and kisses him.* BASIL *leans over and gives her a little kiss on her hair as* TOLLEMACHE *crosses foot of couch, critically examining her feet.*)

LALAGE (*gaily*). Sir Montague, I know you won't believe until you see me walk.

(SIR MONTAGUE *grunts and stands down* L.)

RAGATZY (L. *of couch*). Then he will say he's got on the wrong spectacles.

LALAGE. Oh, no, he won't, he'll render unto Cæsar. I'm going to make them all. You don't know . . . you don't know how good he's been to me. (*Holding out her hand to* RAGATZY.) How gentle, how *wonderful* !

RAGATZY (*taking her hand*). You have said it.

LALAGE.   Yes.   Now take me out of bondage.   Let me go.

RAGATZY.   Yes . . . I set you free.

TOLLEMACHE.   Well, well, no more poetry . . . let's see what she can do.

RAGATZY (*taking coverlet off* LALAGE'S *feet*).   See.   Straight and perfect.   (*Handing wrap to* BASIL.)   If you please, Mr. Owen.

TOLLEMACHE.   Can she bend it ?

LALAGE.   Of course I can.   (*Draws up her knee and clasps it delightedly with both hands.*)

HELMORE.   By Jove, she *can* move it !   (*To* ISRAEL.)

RAGATZY.   It feels all right, hey ?

TOLLEMACHE.   No pain ?

LALAGE.   No.   But so strange ! . . .   (*Stretches it out again.*) Numb.

RAGATZY (C., *briskly*).   You soon get over that.   Now put your foot down.   (*He helps her lift her legs and places them on floor.*)   Now press your foot down.   Now stretch it out.   Very good movement. How do you feel ?

LALAGE.   Strange.

HELMORE (*to* LADD).   Bound to at first.

TOLLEMACHE (*rising and holding her pulse*).   Umph !   You have got too excited.   Did you sleep last night ?

LALAGE (*more naturally*).   No, I couldn't.   I was so happy that it wasn't dark.   The room was full of golden light.

RAGATZY (*moving away from couch*).   Chut chut !   These dreams are only for sick women.   You are well.   In one more minute you rise up and walk.

LALAGE (*dreamily*).   I will arise . . . and go to my father. That's what I was saying all night.   I wrote it to him in a letter that I sent this morning . . . Arise, and go to him.   I think I can stand now.   Let me try.

RAGATZY.   I help you up.   (*He supports her as she slips off the couch and stands.*)   Now you are on the ground.   (*Delighted, moving away from her.*)   Leave go, I tell you.   You are all right.   See, she stands quite straight.

LALAGE (*straightening out her hands to balance*).   I can stand ! How tall I am.

RAGATZY.   How *lovely* !

TOLLEMACHE (*critically*).   She's putting all her weight on the good leg.

RAGATZY (*crossing down* R.C.).   Ah, she is cheating.   Stand fair and square on both feet.   Now walk.

LALAGE (*putting hand to forehead*).   I've forgotten how to.

RAGATZY (*down* R.).   Nonsense, nonsense.   Right foot forward. Right foot, left foot—one foot, two feet.   But you are not moving. Think !   Think !   Send your brain down to your feet !   Walk !

Walk! I tell you. Look at me. Look at me. (*With intensity.*)
You can walk. (*Holds out arms.*) Come to me.

    LALAGE. *I can't.*

(RAGATZY *brusquely motions* BASIL *to take his place.* BASIL *comes
down quickly.*)

    RAGATZY. Bah! You will not. Look at him, then. See, he
holds his arms out for you. Call her, Mr. Owen.

    BASIL (*low and urgent*). Lally, come to me.

    LALAGE (*joyously*). Basil!

(*She takes one step with her good foot, pauses on it an instant. She
takes one step with her left foot, rests on it only an instant, puts her
right foot down firmly and pauses radiantly—then hesitates before
taking a step with the left foot again.* BASIL *makes a little movement
towards her. The doctors strain forward anxiously. She sees the
apprehension in their faces. Puts her left down. She takes a step
but sways, and as the leg gives under her, with a little shriek, falls
forward in a heap at* BASIL'S *feet.*)

    BASIL (*recoils in horror*). LALLY!!!

    RAGATZY (*stunned*). Oh, my God, what have I done! What
have I done!

(SURGEONS *move forward.*)

    TOLLEMACHE (*terribly*). You have destroyed the nerve power!

    BASIL (*at* R. *of* RAGATZY—*screams*). You quack! You damn
quack!

    ISRAEL (*to* BASIL). Sh . . . boy! Don't.

    HELMORE (*cries*). Get her on to the couch.

(BASIL *stumbles into the chair down* R. *muttering:* "My God!"
Collapses.)

(HELMORE *and* LADD *help* RAGATZY *to place* LALAGE *on the couch.*
TOLLEMACHE *stands on left of couch.*)

    RAGATZY (*pushing them aside*). Leave her alone. Now go.

    TOLLEMACHE. No, we are going to take this case out of your
hands.

    RAGATZY. Get out!

    HELMORE (*moving up to* ISRAEL *by couch*). If she tries to walk
again, God only knows what will happen to her.

    RAGATZY. Do you hear me?

    ISRAEL (*moving up to door*). I'll telephone to Sturdee.

    RAGATZY. Yes, send for him. He is the only one who has the
right. Get out, I say, get out, all of you. I am master here.

(ISRAEL *exits, followed by* HELMORE *and* LADD.)

(TOLLEMACHE *stands in door.*)

TOLLEMACHE. Sir, you will have to face her father.

(*Exit* TOLLEMACHE.)

RAGATZY. Get out, get out, I tell you, or so help me Christ!
I'll throw you out from there. (*Turning, goes to* BASIL. *Terribly.*)
And you too get out. You can't stay unless you fight to stay. All
morning you were full of fight, now is the time for it. You don't
want to fight for her now. She is not worth it now. She is a
cripple and you don't want her now . . . (*Stands above chair.*)

BASIL (*with heroic effort*). I'm going to stay. I *have* stayed all
the time.

RAGATZY (*almost shouting*). Why did you stay? Because I
made you.

LALAGE (*roused by his voice, rising on one arm with an exceedingly
bitter cry*). Oh!!!

RAGATZY (*in consternation*). My great God! when you were so
ill I think that if he leave you, all is ended.

BASIL (*crossing to her swiftly*). Lally, I'm going to marry you,
I'm going to just the same!

LALAGE (*working up to helpless hysteria*). But you don't want
to, so I don't want you. Send him away! I can't bear any more!
I can't! Send him *away*!!

RAGATZY. Do you hear! She does not want you. So you go
to hell! Go now!

(BASIL *walks slowly to door and goes out.*)

(RAGATZY *walks heavily to head of couch. Almost collapses, but with
terrific effort gradually pulls himself together, and walks round head
of couch.*)

(*Raises her in his arms and sits* R. *of couch.*) My lovely dear one.
You must understand. I have *not* failed. Muscles never before in
use could not endure the sudden pressure. But your hip, the
crippled hip, is strong as mine. I have cured it. I know it. I am
raging . . . because I hate them so. I could feel the triumph in
their hearts when you fell. But now we're alone. (*Voice changes.*)
The air is clear and strong. Have courage. Now . . . you will
rise up . . . and walk!

LALAGE (*she sits up*). There is still hope?

RAGATZY. Hope! Oh, my dear one, please believe me. Please!

LALAGE. I do! I do!

RAGATZY. Get up! (*She holds hand out as before.*) Now alone!
All alone! (*She rises, hands on couch as before.*) Take your hands
away. (*She takes her hands away.*)

LALAGE. Give me . . . just a moment.

RAGATZY. Stand a moment first!

LALAGE (*thrilled*). Oh, I *do* feel so different.

Ragatzy (*thrilled by her joy*). Oh, thank God, I knew it. Now, come to me. (*Holds his arms out to her* R. *of* C.)

(*With all the confidence in the world, she steps out on her good foot. Her joy increases. She boldly steps out with her other foot ; this time it holds up and her thrill hits the heights, but as her good foot goes out and the other takes the weight, she crumples to the ground. He gazes down at her and she up at him. So sudden was the collapse that they still have the smile of joy in their eyes, causing a hideous paradox. Then very slowly the light goes out, as if what had happened couldn't have happened, until they stare at each other like frozen people. Then still in a daze, he slowly leans down and picks her up in his arms. Stands there in a dead silence, holding her to him like a child, suddenly wounded. And still in the daze he sits her up on the chair down* R. *and stares at her, trying desperately to think, but can't.*)

Lalage (*murmurs*). Why don't you say something ? Is . . . all hope lost ?

Ragatzy (*turning away, starts bravely*). No, no, you will walk. You will . . . you . . . (*Voice dies weakly away.*)

Lalage. No . . . no . . . I won't. I won't—I know I won't. (*A clutch for a straw.*) Will I ?

Ragatzy. I don't know. I . . . My God, have I *done* something that I do not know ! (*Stops. Another pause. Too deeply in love to stand the shock, he is dumbfounded for the first time in his career.*)

Lalage (*trying to realize it*). And . . . just a minute ago—I was sure.

(Ragatzy, *keeping his back to her, suffers hard.*)

(*Trying to rally.*) But, it's all right. I'll get used to it again. It's all right.

Ragatzy (*suddenly faces her, desperately tries to cheer*). Yes, it *is* all right. It *is*. It will gradually come. The tissues . . . will grow slowly stronger and very soon you'll . . .

Lalage (*interrupts passionately*). Don't. I can't bear to hear you. You've failed. Why don't you admit it ? Why don't you tell me I have gone through it for nothing ? All that torture ! A whole year ! For nothing ! And worse still . . . your promises. (*He turns away. She starts to sob hysterically.*) Are you what they say you are ? . . . Are you just a ghastly fraud ? Oh God ! how could you hurt me so ? Oh, God ! (*Gasps with dry sobs.*)

(*He bows his head to the storm.*)

(*She is tearing him to pieces. Calms a little and again implores him.*) Oh . . . but I don't mean that either . . . But I do want a little hope . . . Can't you give me . . . just a little ?

RAGATZY. Not . . . not if I have done the thing that they say. . . . destroyed the nerve power. If . . . if I have done this . . . I . . . I am ended.

LALAGE (*bitterly*). You ? Oh, yes, I forgot. Your reputation was at stake. That's all that matters.

RAGATZY (*broken*). No.

LALAGE. Do you think I have forgotten why you broke into my house ? Because you wanted me for an advertisement. A girl or a dog on the rack . . . what's the difference, so long as you succeed ?

RAGATZY. But if I fail, and if the girl is you . . .

LALAGE. You're wondering now what they are going to say. Oh, your poor pride. Your poor crippled pride . . .

RAGATZY (*faces her for the first time, sharply*). That is not true.

(*She knows it isn't, and drops her eyes.*)

I don't blame you to believe it . . . But it is not true. Yes, I did come to you that way . . . I came to beat them at any cost. You were to be but another step . . . on the way up . . . instead, I find I have reached the summit. Could a man have a greater ambition . . . (*looking out front*) than to make happy the woman that he loves ? Or greater pain than knowing he has tortured her a year . . . just as you say . . . for nothing but more pain ?

LALAGE (*murmurs*). I'm sorry.

RAGATZY (*suddenly furious*). But I don't want you to be sorry. No sympathy. That is the thing I can't stand. I want you to hate me. No pity, for God's sake. No ! (*With his old braggadocio, suddenly pounds self.*) Ragatzy the surgeon has no regrets. I fight a good fight. I did my best. I lose instead of win . . . that's all. (*Touches himself with sudden pathos.*) But the other . . . Me . . . how he does suffer. No torture exists like the sight of your eyes with the light of joy gone out. (*She gazes at him, fascinated by his sudden shifts. He stares at her and his manner changes as his heart leaps. His manner arouses her.*) But oh . . . they are still so beautiful. I promise you shall never see me any more.

LALAGE (*unsteadily*). You said it would be . . . strange . . . never to come again. . . .

RAGATZY. I did not know it would be *terrible*.

LALAGE (*very low*). Where are you going ?

RAGATZY. Outside . . . to meet your father. To let him say what things he will to me.

LALAGE. And then ?

RAGATZY (*kisses her hand with the same passion as he kissed her lips and goes out down U.L.C.*) Good-bye. (*The doors close after him. She sits a moment motionless, then looking up realizes he is gone.*)

LALAGE. No, no . . . don't go. Please don't go. (*Rising desperately, not realizing she has risen.*) Come back. Come back !

I love you. I don't believe that you have failed! I can't believe it! (*Pointing to hall.*) Call him! Call him!

(*In the middle of the room she sways, but this time she doesn't fall. This causes her to realize she has walked and she stares back at the distance to couch and then down at her feet. She passes her hand across her forehead.*)

(*As this is happening* Nurse *is heard calling* Ragatzy, *who appears at hall door, has been told by* Nurse *she stands, but the shock is almost as great as the sight of her. They stare at each other. Then she slowly goes across room to him, they clasp each other. Then, overcome, he falls on one knee at her feet. He clasps her knees and lays his face against her. She puts a tender hand on his bowed head, lifting her radiant face in thankfulness to Heaven.*)

The Curtain *falls.*

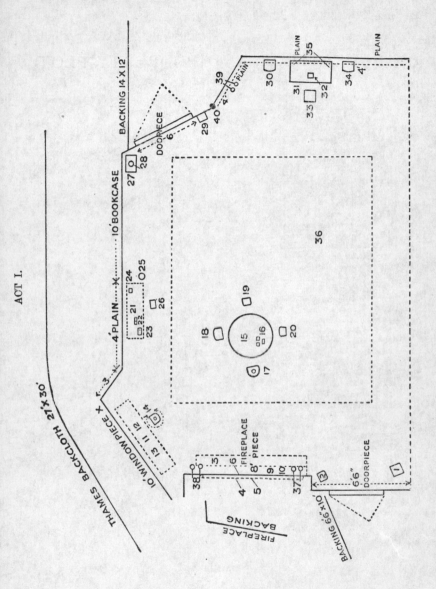

ACT I.

75

FURNITURE AND PROPERTY PLOT

ACT 1.

1. Green plush armchair.
2. Mahogany armchair.
3. Club fender.
4. Mantelpiece.
5. Fireplace.
6. Oil Painting.
7. Clock ⎫
8. Bronzes ⎬ on mantelpiece.
9. Directory ⎭
10. Ashtray.
11. Sofa table.
12. Revolving bookcase.
13. Papers, magazines on table.
14. Revolving armchair.
15. Round table with
16. Books and magazines on, etc.
17. Revolving armchair.
18. Oak armchair.
19. Small wooden chair.
20. Wooden chair.
21. Walnut bureau.
22. Two-well inkstand.
23. Pens, blotter, papers, etc.
24. Standard lamp and shade.
25. Waste-paper basket.
26. Small wooden chair.
27. Pedestal column.
28. Bronze " Napoleon."
29. House telephone.
30. Small wooden chair.
31. Mahogany secular bookcase.
32. Attache-case.
33. Small wooden chair.
34. Small wooden chair.
35. Papers, letters, etc.
36. Large red carpet.
37. Electric light bracket.
38. Electric light bracket.
39. Electric light bracket.
40. Light switch.

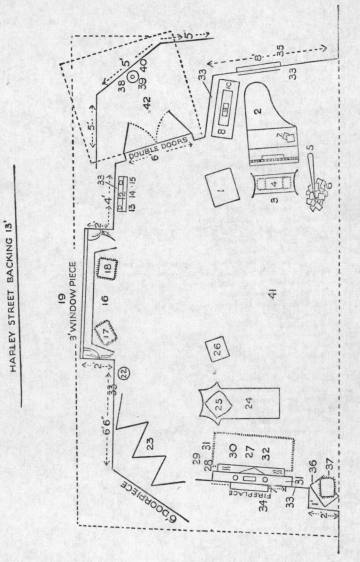

DOUBLE DOORS

3' WINDOW PIECE

6' DOORPIECE

FIREPLACE

ACT II

1. Small blue tapestry chair.
2. Baby grand piano.
3. Black and gold lacquer piano stool.
4. Oblong silver bolster.
5. Crutch.
6. MSS. songs and music.
7. "School for Scandal" MSS.
8. Black lacquer cabinet.
9. White marble clock.
10. Blue Chinese embroidery.
11. Cartwheel mahogany armchair.
12. Black and gold lacquer cabinet.
13. Two silver candlesticks.
14. Silver inkstand and ashtray.
15. Blotter and penholder.
16. Long black and gold settee.
17. Silver cushion.
18. Black and silver cushion.
19. Bronze statue (small).
20. Orange net curtains with brackets and rods.
21. Green and gold curtains with pelmet board and pelmet.
22. Lac standard lamp shade.
23. Six-fold Chinese screen.
24. Black and gold tapestry sofa.
25. Silver cushion.
26. Small black lac chair.
27. White sheepskin rug.
28. Set of fire irons.
29. Brass fender.
30. Lac fire screen.
31. Two blue and jade bowls.
32. Sleeping "Buhudda" stand.
33. Set of five Japanese prints.
34. Large oil painting.
35. Large oil painting.
36. Blue tapestry armchair.
37. Black and silver cushion.
38. Black pedestal.
39. Green stone jar.
40. Yellow roses.
41. Large black felt.
42. Red carpet.

Off stage :—
   box of chocolates.
   Bouquet of roses.

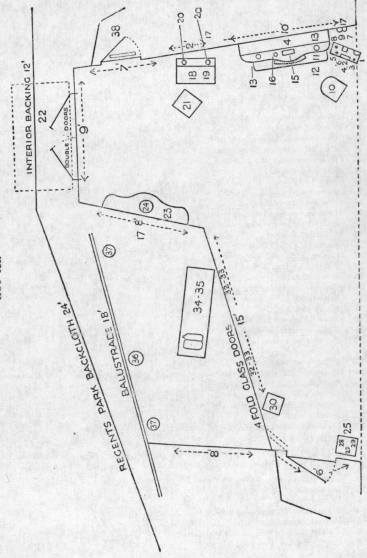

3rd Monday. 1st Tuesday. 3rd Thursd

Next Week.

Monday Sep. 12th.
1st Act.
7-30. all.

Tuesday
2nd act.
7-o-clock
Mac. Sheila. Ethel.

Thursday
3rd act.
7-o-clock
Mac. Sheila. Leslie.

ACT III

cushion for basket chair.

1. Mahogany writing-table.
2. Blotter.
3. Ashtray.
4. Silver cigarette-box.
5. Silver match-box.
6. Special letters.
7. Standard table lamp.
8. Vase of carnations.
9. Bronze figure.
10. Blue wooden armchair.
11. Fire screen.
12. Fender and fireirons.
13. Pair of blue Chinese jars.
14. Large antique oil painting.
15. Ormolu clock.
16. Vase of lilac.
17. 3 hall brackets.
18. Walnut bureau.
19. Letters, papers and etceteras.
20. Pair of blue candlesticks.
21. Walnut chair.
22. Carpet.
23. Green and gold sideboard.
24. Basket of iris.
25. Walnut table.
26. Chinese embroidery.
27. Silver clock.
28. Hand bell.
29. Book of poems.
30. Yellow painted chair.
31. 2 pairs of cream silk curtains.
32. 4 pairs of curtain brackets.
33. 4 pairs of white rods.
34. Medical jack with 2 sheets, 2 pillows, 2 pillow-slips, head-rest, 4 wooden blocks.
35. Green silk Chinese shawl.
36. Standard floor lamp, 2 shades.
37. 2 tubs with plants.
38. Oval oil paintings—Acts II and III.

Used only in scene II and not shown on the plan. Full instructions are given in the stage directions at the beginning of this scene.

1. Couch with blue Chinese cover.
2. 7 baskets of flowers.
3. Round blue table.
4. 2 black and grey cushions.
5. Round black cushion.
6. Yellow Chinese dragon shawl (silk).
7. Small marble top stool.

Sheila. That's what I dont know.

Malcolm. I let him kiss